AF559631

Hindus Under Siege:

The Way Out

BY THE SAME AUTHOR

Ayodhya: Ram Temple and Hindu Rennaissance

The Ideology of India's Modern Right

Sri Lanka in Crisis: India's Options

Rama Setu: Symbol of National Unity

Economic Development and Reforms in India and China

Corruption and Corporate Governance in India: Satyam, Spectrum and Sundaram

Hindutva and National Renaissance

India's China Strategic Perspective

Virat Hindu Identity: Concept and its Power

Building the Sri Rama Temple in Ayodhya

2G Spectrum Scam

Terrorism in India

Human Rights and Terrorism in India

The Hindu Manifesto for India's Democracy

Hindus Under Siege:
The Way Out

Subramanian Swamy, Ph.D. (Harvard)

Member of Parliament, India
Former Union Cabinet Minister for
Commerce, Law & Justice, India

HAR-ANAND
PUBLICATIONS PVT LTD

Dedicated to ...
The memory of and the wisdom of
Sri Parmacharya, Chandrashekhera, Saraswathi,
Jagadguru Shankaracharya,
Kanchi Mutt.

Reprint, 2023

Published by Ashok Gosain and Ashish Gosain for
HAR-ANAND PUBLICATIONS PVT LTD
E-49/3, Okhla Industrial Area, Phase-II, New Delhi-110020
Tel: 41603490
E-mail: info@haranandbooks.com/haranand@rediffmail.com
Shop online at: www.haranandbooks.com

Printed in India

For want of knowledge,
Wisdom was lost
For want of wisdom,
Character was lost
For want of character,
Momentum was lost
For want of momentum,
Wealth was lost
For want of wealth,
The down-trodden were lost.
All for want of knowledge was lost.

—*Mahatma Jyotiba Phule*

IF

If you can keep your head when all about you
Are losing theirs and blaming it on you,
If you can trust yourself when all men doubt you,
But make allowance for their doubling too,
If you can wait and not be tired by waiting,
Or being lied about, don't deal in lies,
Or being hated don't give way to hating,
And yet don't look too good, nor talk too wise;
If you can dream and not make dreams your master
If you can think and not make thoughts your aim,
If you can meet with Triumph and Disaster
And treat those two imposters just the same;
If you can bear to hear the truth you've spoken
Twisted by knaves to make a trap for fools,
Or watch the things you gave your life to, broken,
And stoop and build' em up with worn-out tools;
If you can make one heap of all your winnings
And risk it on one turn of pitch-and-toss,
And lose, and start again at your beginnings
And never breathe a word about your loss,
If you can force your heart and nerve and sinews
To serve your turn long after they are gone
And so hold on when there is nothing in you
Except the Will which says to them: "Hold on!"
If you can talk with crowds and keep your virtue,
Or walk with Kings—nor lose the common touch,
If neither foes nor loving friends can hurt you,
If all men count with you, but none too much;
If you can fill the unforgiving minute
With sixty seconds' worth of distance run,
Yours is the Earth and everything that's in it,
And—which is more—you'll be a Man, my son!

—Rudyard Kipling

Preface

In 1971, after nearly a decade of scholarship and teaching economics at Harvard University, I returned to India and published a best-seller *Indian Economic Planning—An Alternative Approach*. In public platforms thereafter, I began propagating an alternative economic strategy for India that called for adopting a market economy, for restructuring our foreign policy to befriend the US, Israel and China and thus diluting our dependence on USSR. That ideological package was heavily condemned then by the Left-dominated academia. But the unraveling of the USSR and the adoption of pro-market reforms by communist China have now completely undermined the Left intellectual position. My views have, therefore, become mainstream.

Since becoming free of British Imperialist rule in 1947, India's ideological space had been for five decades circumscribed by a Left-leaning socialist secular framework, with very little room left in the mainstream of thought for any other significantly different ideological perspective. Because of a dominant government controlling the commanding heights of the economy, ruled by a party that became increasingly authoritarian, any serious secular ideological challenge to this established thought was crushed at the nascent stage. Even when the nation faced a grave economic crisis, as in 1991, that required some dismantling of the oppressive regulatory system, it was dressed up as a reform and a natural evolution of the same framework. But the author of this reform who dared to deviate more than necessary, namely, Prime Minister Narasimha Rao, was disowned by his party and the Left, and then was pilloried, defamed and criminally prosecuted till his heart gave out. Even in his last rites, he was not honoured. Instead he was made an example of, for others who doubted this Left-leaning socialist secular framework.

In this suffocating atmosphere, only a right wing religious radical formation could find a footing, and which gradually expanded onto the center stage of the national ideological platform. But within six years of being in power and office, that too fizzled out because of the leadership's inexplicable reluctance to make a clean and clear break with the past failed ideological framework.

Both the Left-leaning secular Socialists and the Capitulationist Right have had their innings, and are unlikely to regain the center stage. What remains today in the country is an ideological mish-mash. Till a new ideological framework is designed and presented with clarity to the people, the present hybrid ideological *ad hocism* will continue. This confused state of affairs cannot steer the nation to new heights of economic development, a more cohesive nation, and world power status.

To research, propound, and propagate a new ideological framework that can unite the nation, make the people strive to global greatness and struggle for world power, the Centre for National Renaissance has been set up in New Delhi to be funded by the Naveen Hindustan Trust. My colleagues and I, who constitute the Centre's Board of Governors, have an established and acknowledged record of dissenting from the past ideological framework of the nation. This dissent has sometimes taken the form of struggle and for this we have suffered: the state has denied us our due in our professional life. We also were denounced as conservatives or reactionaries. But we never wavered, convinced that the day will dawn when an alternative ideology of national renaissance or modern conservatives will be needed by the Country. The new millennium holds that promise. We need, therefore, to have a clear understanding of an agenda for renaissance.

At the present juncture of our history, if we are to pick up the thread of renaissance from where it had been snapped in 1947, and from where Swami Vivekananda, Maharishi Aurobindo and Mahatma Gandhi had brought it, *we need first to define a new agenda*, and then build a suitable vehicle to implement that agenda to its fruition. For that we have to be clear about the fundamentals of Indian identity, and of renaissance itself.

Is there a need for such an agenda? In the absence of a well-articulated and well-thought through agenda, there will always be in circulation, a defunct or a haphazard one. Those who decry the need for an explicit and positive agenda are usually slaves of defunct ones. The Morarji Desai Government had such an unarticulated agenda. It consisted of four points: Prohibition, Ban on Cow-slaughter, Freedom of Religion Bill, and Revision of History Textbooks. None of the points of this agenda were inherently bad, but because the *raison d'etre,* or the fundamental premise of the agenda was not to raise the consciousness of the people but to pursue it as a law and order matter, the implicit Desai agenda came into disrepute and was then denounced as retrograde by Leftists in India, who are neurotic about any move to usher in anything resembling Hindu renaissance. During her long reign of 16 years, Mrs. Indira Gandhi too was an adherent of an implicit agenda which was a mixture of Mrs. Gandhi's own *noblesse oblige*, and superstitious belief in tantrik practices. During Mrs. Gandhi's reign, the so called God-men *astrologers* and *Yagna* performers proliferated, and thus the agenda boiled down to merely fossilizing existing religious practices and caste structures, and to deepening superstitious beliefs. During Mrs. Gandhi's reign we got the worst of both worlds. On the one hand we failed to foster a positive attitude towards our heritage and civilization, and on the other hand we strengthened bodies which inculcated the narrow and obscurantist interpretation of living Hindu wisdom.

The lesson to be drawn from our past experience thus is that either India explicitly will have to adopt an agenda and make dynamic progress, or suffer an implicit defunct agenda, which will invariably be retrograde, and weaken the country. The items on this Agenda will constitute the Indian identity and goals, and will foster the renaissance. No nation can survive for long without a binding identity concept. Why was Akhand Hindustan partitioned in 1947? Or Pakistan split in 1971? Or the USSR disintegrated in 1991? Or Yugoslavia balkanised in 1996? Or, alternatively why were Germany [1989] and Vietnam [1975] re-united? A common history, language structures, folklore, and a common perception of the same, of the people, binds them into a nation. A lack of it divides nations, sooner or later.

What are then the items of such an Agenda which can have national support of patriots and yet usher in a renaissance? How much of this renaissance will be for Hindus, and in how much of it can the minorities participate without feeling insecure or threatened? How can a consensus shape clarity in the concept of an Indian identity? These are crucial questions I hope to answer in the chapters of this book. Those opposed to a vibrant patriotic bonding of Indians will, no doubt, find much of what I say as 'Chauvinist' and 'Conservative' but I own the epithets. Nothing I say will satisfy them because these critics such as communists are 'guided,' and even controlled, by foreign ideologies and interests. Others may disagree and want to debate the issues. I welcome these others.

What does it ideologically mean to be a conservative? Conservatives do not promise to create heaven on earth. We know that to be an idle utopia. Instead conservatives promise change while preserving the best in our past. As conservatives we dare to change the things that we must and can, and await the moment when we can change that which we must but which we cannot for now. The wisdom of the ideology lies in delineating possibilities. But we are for consistent, if only gradual, change brought about by the individual himself driven by his own enlightened interests in the milieu of voluntary social actions and norms. We do believe that the individual can be, and should be, motivated by incentives, by equipping him with fundamental concepts of his individual, social and national identity, empowered by adequate education, and a democratic temper.

The ideological framework of conservatism to achieve national renaissance, which thus the Centre proposes to research, articulate and propagate in an intellectually challenging way, has the following markers:

(*a*) The state is to be *minimalist* in regulatory interventions in social and economic matters, *maximalist* in the maintenance of law & order, in opposing terrorism, and *optimalist* in providing the quality of life needs, while being politically accountable to the people in a democracy.

(*b*) A social ethos based on the concepts of trusteeship of wealth, philanthropy and voluntary group action is encouraged by religious sanction for the better distribution of income and for minimizing economic contradictions and deprivation.

(*c*) The key goal of the state is to empower the individual through a modern education that blends the essential concepts of spiritual commitment with material pursuits to enable the individual to be self-reliant and yet have strong character.

(*d*) The individual is to be persuaded by the state by incentives and not by coercion. Hence, the state will make no promise to the people without specifying the sacrifices to be made.

(*e*) India can make rapid economic progress to become a developed country only through a globally competitive economy that requires assured access to the markets and technological innovations of the United States and its allies. This has concomitant political obligations that must be accepted as essential for national renaissance.

(*f*) Such rapid progress would require a national security strategy for securing a peaceful environment which necessitates strong security ties with India's neighbours and with such of those countries with which India has no intrinsic clash of interests.

(*g*) At present, Indians in general and especially the Hindus who constitute over 80 percent of the nation, have loyalty to the family but are apathetic to the community where they live. The Indian does not easily acknowledge the accomplishment of other Indians. He respects intellectual endeavour but not dignity of labour, and is more concerned with form of behaviour than content of his commitment. Moreover, the higher he rises in authority the less does an Indian feel accountable for his actions. These character flaws have come to be acquired from two centuries of deprivation but are incompatible with a people desiring to be a great nation; and they can be rectified by developing a strong and coherent concept of national identity whose defining characteristics can be culled from a correct perception of our history and our religious traditions embodied in *Sanatana Dharma*.

This is an enormous but glorious task, that calls for ushering in a renaissance in the national outlook and mindset. The Centre for National Renaissance, therefore, seeks ties with other like-minded institutions, think tanks, and international conservative foundations to benefit from their experience and thus be enabled to perform this momentous task.

This book is therefore, written to inform the dimensions of possible research for future scholars and those of the Centre. Although the views expressed herein are the author's, nevertheless the broad ideological framework in the chapters of the book are the *raison d'etre* of the Centre.

In writing this book I was admirably assisted in the research and editing of the manuscript by my wife Dr. Roxna S. Swamy, who is however not responsible for the remaining errors.

DR. SUBRAMANIAN SWAMY

Contents

1.

Introduction

The Concept of an Indian Identity and Mindset

Since achieving independence from colonial rule in 1947, we Indians have been unsuccessfully grappling with the following question: Who are we? Are we? *This as—yet unanswered question represents India's identity crisis.* The failure to date to resolve this crisis, has not only confused the majority but has also confounded the minorities as well in India. Without a resolution of this crisis, (which requires an explicit, clear answer to the question), the majority will never understand how to relate to the legacy of the nation. In other words, the present dysfunctional perceptional mismatch, between who we are as a people and the legacy of the nation, is behind most of the communal tension and inter-community distrust in the country. Even in other countries such a question arises from time to time. In the United States, following relatively liberal immigration policies since 1965, the question has again arisen. Prof. Samuel Huntington of Harvard has tried to answer this question in his new book: *Who We Are?*

What is India; and why are we Indians? Is India an ancient nation, a continuing civilization of thousands of years, or is it a relatively recent administrative construct of British imperialists and legalized by the British House of Commons legislation, viz., *The Indian Independence Act of 1947*? What is the core of India's ethos; Hindu,

Secular or Hindustani? And what does each mean? Citizens of modern India are of course not sure! That is today's identity crisis.

Unless we answer this question clearly, finally, unambiguously, and authoritatively as to who we are, Indians will flounder, flip-flop, and generally be devoid of healthy patriotism. This is not to suggest that any person's identity is uni-dimensional. The nature of a person's questioning mind in a pluralistic democracy makes identity a multi-dimensional concept. But a national identity dimension is an imperative for a nation to become vibrant and dynamic. What we are concerned with here is the lack of a national identity, *not* how to make such an identity the sole concern. When the nation is in danger, national identity must take precedence. That is what Chanakya meant by the concept of a "Chakravartin".

The core fundamentals of our national identity, through a correct perception of our history, will help to restructure and reform our society on that basis and will make it cohesive and united. To achieve such a restructure, of course, requires a complete de-falsification of Indian history, rejecting that portion that has been deliberately contrived by British imperialists and their Indian compradors, to snap the linkages to our real past.

The present history taught in our schools and colleges is still the British-imperialist sponsored one, in which India as a State is treated as of recent origin and British-created. The Indian people are portrayed as a heterogeneous lot who are hopelessly divided against themselves. Both caste and language differences are given an ethnic interpretation.

Such a "history" had without doubt been British policy. Sir George Hamilton, Secretary of State for India, wrote on March 26, 1888 that "I think the real danger of our rule is not now but say 50 years hence ..... We shall (therefore) break Indians into two sections holding widely different views ..... We should so plan the educational text books that the differences between community and community are further strengthened". Dr. B.R. Ambedkar challenged this view as far back as 1916, when, as a doctoral student of economics at Columbia University, he wrote a paper for an Anthropology Department seminar as follows: "Ethnically, all people are heterogeneous. It is the unity of culture that is the basis of homogeneity. Taking this for granted, I venture to say that there is no country that can rival the Indian Peninsula with respect to unity. It has not only geographic unity, but it has over and above all a deeper and much more fundamental unity – the indubitable cultural unity that covers the land from end to end [Published in Indian Antiquary, Vol. XLI, May 1917, p. 94].

After achieving independence, under the leadership of Jawaharlal Nehru and the implementing authority of the ICS, de-falsification of our history was never done, in fact the very idea was condemned as "obscuranist" and Hindu chauvinist. For a brief period, when Murli Manohar Joshi was in charge of the Education portfolio at the Centre (1998-2004) an attempt was made to de-falsify history. But again it was done not by challenging scholarly debate, but by changing textbooks on government diktat, *i.e.*, putting the 'cart before the horse'. The effort became tainted as 'saffronisation'. Joshi had got it right conceptually, but he got poor support from his colleagues in government for implementing it. It was not given priority.

What is the gist of this British imperialist-tailored Indian history? In this history, India is portrayed as the land conquered first by the Dravidians, then by the Aryans, later by Muslims, and finally by the British. Our history books today portray this obsession with foreign rule. For example, even though the Mughal rule from Akbar to Aurangzeb is about 150 years, *much shorter than the 350 year rule of the Vijayanagaram empire,* the history books of today hardly take notice of the latter. In fact the territory under Krishna Devaraya's rule was much larger than Akbar's, and yet it is the latter who is called "the Great". Such a version suited the British rulers who had sought thereby to create a legitimacy for their presence in India. Furthermore, we were also made to see advantages accruing from British rule, the primary one being that India was created by this colonialism; that but for the British, India would never have been a country, that we were freed from superstition and obscurantism by the colonisers and given a 'modern' education to boot.

These totally false and pernicious ideas have permeated deep into our educational system. They have poisoned the minds of our younger generations who have not had the benefit of the freedom struggle to awaken their pride and nationalism. It has thus to be an essential part of the renaissance agenda that the two ideas of British-sponsored history of India are discarded, namely: (1) that India as a State was a gift of the British and (2) that there is no such thing as a native Indian, and what we are today is a by-product of the rape of the land by visiting conquerors and their hordes.

Just because India did not have a nation state of the present boundaries, exercising control through a unified modern administration, does not mean that there was no India. On the contrary, there was always an India, which, from north to south, thought fundamentally as one country. Just as Hinduism exists from ancient days despite a lack of a 'Church, Book, or Pope', Hindustan too existed from time immemorial but without the paraphernalia of a modern state.

The British on the contrary tried to disrupt that unity by destroying the traditional communication channels and structures, and demeaning India's heritage by falsification and disinformation.

Thus, we need a new factual account of our history, focusing on the continuous and unbroken endeavours of a people united as a nation. This history of India must deal with the conscious effort of our people to achieve a civilization, to reach better standards of life, and live a happier and nobler life. The lamp of faith of the Indian people burned brightly over a long period. We must also record when that faith dimmed in our history and brought shame to the people. Such a factual account of our past is essential to the Agenda, because we have to disgorge and discard the foreign versions of our history with credibility. It is this foreign version that makes us foreigners in our own land. The Aryan-Dravidian divide in the history taught in schools and universities is purely a conception of foreign historians like Max Mueller; and it has no basis in Indian historical records. This fraudulent history has been lapped up by many upper caste Indians, as their racial passport to Europe. Such has been the demoralization of the Hindu mind, which we have to shake off through a new factual account of our past.

The theory of the Aryan invasion, which is still taken by some as the foundation stone of the history of India, was actually devised in the 18th and 19th centuries by British linguists and archaeologists. According to this theory the first inhabitants of India were good-natured, peaceful, dark-skinned shepherds, called the Dravidians, who had founded what is called the Harappan, Indus Valley civilization. They were supposedly remarkable builders—witness the city of Mohenjo-Daro in Pakistani Sind, but had no culture to speak of, no literature, no proper script even. Around 1500 B.C., India is said to have been invaded by tribes called the Aryans: white-skinned, nomadic people, who originated somewhere in Western Russia and imposed upon the Dravidians the hateful caste system. To the Aryans are attributed Sanskrit and the Vedas, the Vedic or Hindu religious spiritual texts, as well as a host of subsequent writings, the Upanishads, the Mahabharata, the Ramayana, etc.

By this 'Aryan' theory, the British showed on the one hand that Indian civilization was not that ancient and that it was posterior to the cultures which influenced the Western world – Mesopotamia, Sumeria, or Babylon – and that whatever good things India had developed-Sanskrit literature, or even its architecture – had been borrowed from, or influenced by the West. Thus, Sanskrit, instead of being the mother of all Indo-European languages, became just a branch of their huge family. The religion of Zarathustra is said to have influenced Hinduism, and not vice versa. And on the other hand, it divided India and pitted against each other the 'low caste dark-skinned Dravidians' and the 'high caste light-skinned Aryans', a rift which is still enduring.

But today, this theory is being challenged by two new discoveries, one archaeological and the other linguistic. Firstly, in the Rig Veda, the Ganges, India's sacred river, is only mentioned once, but the mythical Saraswati is praised fifty times. For a long time, the Saraswati river was indeed considered a myth, until the American satellite Landstat was able to photograph and map the bed of this magnificent river, and trace its source in the Himalayas. Archaeologist Paul-Henri Francfort, who studied the Saraswati region at the beginning of the Nineties, found that the Saraswati had "disappeared", because around 2200 BC, an immense drought reduced the whole region to aridity and famine. "Thus", he writes, "most inhabitants moved away from the Saraswati to settle on the banks of the Indus and Sutlej rivers". According to 'official' history, the Vedas were composed around 1500 BC, some even say 1200 BC. Yet, the Rig Veda describes India as it was before the great drought which dried up the Saraswati, which means in effect that the so called Indus, or Harappan, civilization, was a continuation of the Vedic epoch, which ended approximately when the Saraswati dried up.

There is, however, no such word as 'Aryan' in Sanskrit literature [closest is 'arya' meaning honourable person, and not a community]. The word "Dravidian" was coined by Adi Sankara, a Brahmin monk from Kerala: in his *shasthrath* with Mandana Mishra at Varanasi, he had called himself a 'Dravida shishu' that is a child of an area where three oceans meet, *i.e.*, south India]. The north-south racial divide theory was thus a deliberate distortion by British imperialists and propagated by their witting and unwitting, mentally enslaved

Indian scholars. Incidentally, the Aryan-Dravidian myth has now been exploded by modern research on DNA of Indians and Europeans conducted by Professor C. Panse of Newton, Mass. USA and other scholars. In light of such new research, the British Broadcasting Corporation [BBC] service, in it's October 6, 2005 service, completely debunked the Aryan—Dravidian race theory stating that: "Theory was not just wrong; it included unacceptably racist ideas" [www.bbc.co.uk, religion & ethics homepage, Thursday, 6-10-2005].

Sri Aurobindo wrote seven decades ago that "Indian scholars have not been able to form themselves into a great and independent school of learning due to two causes: the miserable scantiness of the mastery in Sanskrit provided by our universities, crippling to all but born scholars, and our lack of study independence which makes us over-ready to defer to European [and Western] authority." How true it is even today!

The history of no free country can be structured on foreign accounts of it. The time has come for us to take seriously our Puranic sources and to imbibe a de-falsified and well-founded history of ancient India, a history written by Indians about Indians. Such a history would bring out the amazing continuity of a nation, which nation asserted its identity again and again at times of war and political crises. It should focus on the fact that at the centre of our perception of the Indian nation, is the concept of the *Chakravartin* ideal—The Chakravartin to be overall in charge to defend the nation from external aggression while giving maximum internal autonomy to the *janapadas*. A correct, defalsified history would record that Hindustan was conceptually one in the art of governance, in the style of royal courts, in the methods of warfare, in the maintenance of its agrarian base, and in the dissemination of information. Otherwise it was decentralized: Villages were self-administered. The Panchayat system is a manifestation of that.

An accurate history, of course, should not only record the periods of glory but the moments of degeneration, of the missed opportunities, and of the failure to forge national unity at crucial junctures in time when it was required to confront and defeat foreign aggressors. It should draw lessons for the future generations from costly disunity errors in the past, for example when Baji Rao and Nizam-ul-Mulk failed to join forces to defeat Nadir Shah in 1739. Similarly, Madhav Rao (Scindhia) and Haider Ali together could have crushed the corrupt East India Company, but Mahadaji Scindhia failed to help Tipu Sultan against Cornwallis. Thereby India was thoroughly defeated and conquered. The same Cornwallis who miserably failed in the American War of Independence in the eighteenth century was able to subdue the much larger population of India because of our inability to close ranks against the foreigner. Thus, it was not the much portrayed Hindu "submission" that was responsible for our subjugation but lack of unity and effective military strategy in a time of decadence and moral decay that had weakened our national resolve.

Therefore, without such an accurate de-falsified history, India cannot develop the correct identity.

The correct perception of Indian identity, briefly stated, is that we are a people who have always constituted a nation, living in a geographical location, spanning from Kashmir to Kanyakumari, from Attak to Car Nicobar, bound together in a continuing civilization of more than 10,000 years, a people who are mostly of Hindu religious faith and of those others of separate, equally respected faiths but whose ancestors are Hindu. There are still others, such as Parsis and Jews, who came as refugees and accepted the culture of Hindus while retaining their religion. They have lived without persecution and never felt the need to demand reservations and quotas for themselves. That is how the Indian evolved. Those who acknowledge this legacy are modern Indians or Hindustani.

Without a correct perception of our identity in history, India cannot achieve a renaissance. That perception is that the subcontinent of what the world knew as India is the cradle of Hindu civilization, and that while others may have come in sporadic migrations, the civilization became inclusive but the core remained the same: Hindu. That is our identity. We are, will remain at the core, and continue to be globally recognized as a Hindu civilization, which the nation state must represent and fiercely defend.

While the identity thus stated must be unambiguous, nevertheless for it to become vibrant and virile, it is essential that the conceptualization takes the form of a mindset of the Indian. Such a mindset should become an intrinsic part of the ethos of the nation.

The challenge for the coming century—for India to revive itself as a nation and a culture—is to recreate the India model of education in the modern context, in which the dichotomy between science and religion is resolved. We must move beyond not only dogmatic and exclusive religions on the one hand, but also materialistic science on the other. We must recreate religion as a form of science and science as a form of spirituality.

On a practical level this means that the spiritual heritage of India—the Vedas, Upanishads, Yoga and Vedanta and Buddhism—must be taught in the schools as an integral part not only of Indian culture but of the global heritage of spiritual sciences. Sanskrit, the language that is the vehicle for most of these great teachings, therefore must also be given emphasis and its teaching made compulsory.

This requires a new intelligentsia in India, that takes pride in ancient Hindu concepts and ceases to blindly imitate Western models of thinking in the name of modernization. It also requires that the religious institutions, temples and ashrams offer classes on Vedic science, Hindu culture and their modern adaptation. Indian identity has to be rooted in Hinduism. This is possible only if every Indian understands the foundations of Hindu philosophy.

The Concept of Hindustan

Hinduism, known as *sanatana dharma* is unique in that in all the world, it has had a continuous and unbroken tradition for the longest time; and it is a religion constituted by its theology, cultural ethos, and civilizational history. India's Hindu society is founded on the content of these three constituents. Hindustan, as India is known abroad even today [*e.g.*, Yindu guo in Chinese, Hind in Arabic], as a concept is defined as a nation of Hindus and those others in the nation who accept that their ancestors are Hindus and revere that legacy. Parsis, Jews, Syrian Christians come in a special category of Hindustanis, those who were welcomed by Hindus since they came to our country seeking refuge from persecution in their own lands abroad, and who willingly accepted to abide by, and adopt certain cultural customs of Hindus. To the credit of Parsis, they have never demanded any special privileges as a minority. They had even rejected privileges and quotas offered to them by the British imperialists saying that they were comfortable with Hindus.

The Hindu ethos provided a sanctuary and home to those of other faiths fleeing from their countries due to religious persecution. Parsis, Jews and Syrian Christians are among those religious groups who had sought refuge in India, and survived because the Hindus looked after them. These three religious communities have had (and have today) a disproportionate share in power and wealth in Indian society, but Hindus have no resentment about this. These minorities had come to India in search of peace, and they found a safe haven in the midst of Hindu society. Parsis migrated elsewhere in the world too, but disappeared as a community in those countries; Jews have openly acknowledged that India is the only country where they were not persecuted. Syrian Christians too are today completely integrated into India. Even early Arab Muslim travelers who came peacefully to settle in Kerala were taken into Hindu families, and hence called Mapillai [meaning son-in-law—

Moplah in English]. That is the glorious Hindu tradition, the ethos of compassion and co-option that is unparalleled in world history.

However, militant Islam and later crusading Christianity came to India, and aggressively challenged Hinduism. They seized power in sequence and established their own state in India. But despite state patronage to the ensuing onslaught, plunder and victimisation, those of Hindu faith could not be decimated, and Hinduism remained the theology of the vast Indian majority.

The true factual history is that defiant Hindus suffered persecution and economic deprivation during Islamic and Christian reigns, such as through differential taxation [*e.g.*, jizia and zamindari land revenue appropriation] and plain brutality, but Hindus by and large refused to capitulate and convert. Even after almost a thousand years of such targeting by Muslims and Christian rulers, undivided India in 1947 was more than 75% Hindu. This was partly because of the victorious Vijayanagaram empire, the Sikh reign, and Mahratta kingdoms, and later the Freedom Movement, each inspired by sanyasis such as Sringeri Shankaracharya, Swami Ramdas, Guru Nanak, Swami Vivekananda and Sri Aurobindo, who by their preaching about the Hindu identity ensured that the flame of Hindu defiance never dimmed. It was also due to individual defiance of Hindus such as Rana Pratap, Rani Jhansi, Rani Bennur, Kattaboman and Netaji Subhas Bose. These icons are admired not because they led us to victory [in fact they were defeated or killed], or had found out a safe compromise [they did not], but because of their courage of conviction in the face of huge odds not to submit to tyranny. That courageous defiance is also a part of Hinduism's glorious legacy. But those who capitulated like Raja Man Singh or Jai Chand or Pudukottai Raja, in order to live in pomp and grandeur are despised today by the people. These legacies need to form the mindset of the modern Hindu.

What exactly is today confronting Hindus, is however, much more difficult to meet than earlier in history because the forces at work to erode and undermine Hindu faith, unlike before, are unseen, clandestine, pernicious, deceptive but most of all sophisticated and media-savvy. Tragically therefore, a much more educated and larger numbers of Hindus have been unwittingly co-opted today in this sinister conspiracy directed by foreigners who have no love for India and who also see (much as Lord Macaulay saw in the nineteenth century), that the hoary Hindu foundation of India is a stumbling block for the furtherance of their nefarious perfidious game.

Adherence to Hinduism is also being sought to be diluted in the name of modernity and this dilution is made a norm of secularism. Religion, it is advocated, is personal. To be a good Hindu today is conceptually being reduced to just praying, piety, visiting temples, and celebrating religious festivals. The concept of a collective Hindu mindset is being ridiculed as chauvinist and retrograde, even fundamentalist.

The concept of a corporate Hindu unity and identity however is that of a collective mindset that identifies us with a motherland from the Himalayas to the Indian Ocean and it's glorious past, *and* the concomitant resolve of it's representative leadership (earlier defined by Chanakya as "chakravartin"), to defend that vision. It is this concept and resolve that is being discarded or is just evaporating under the onslaught of the Nehruvian secularists.

However pious a Hindu becomes, however prosperous Hindu temples become from the offerings of devotees, when the nation is in peril it is only this collective mindset of the people that matters, and not the piety of some individual.

Lacking a cohesive corporate identity, Hindu society today is in the process of becoming fragmented, and hence increasingly in disarray. This fission process is on simultaneously with the reality of millions of Hindus who go regularly to temples or to places of pilgrimage like Sabarimalai or to the Kumbh Mela. This is not what I mean by Hindu unity.

I am instead referring to the Hindu consciousness which encompasses the willingness and determination to collectively defend the faith from the erosion that is being induced by the disconnect with our glorious past. What Swami Vivekananda, Bankim Chatterjee, Sri Aurobindo, and Subramaniya Bharati had achieved by raising Hindu consciousness to that end, has now been depleted and dissipated over the last six decades.

If this degeneration and disconnect are not rectified and repaired by a resolve to unite Hindustanis [Hindus and those of other faith who proudly accept that their ancestors are Hindus, and who thus identify with India's Hindu past], Hindu civilization may go into a tail spin and ultimately fade away as other civilizations have—and for much the same reason.

Of course, this sorry state has come about as a cumulative effect of a thousand years of Islamic invasions, occupation and Imperialist colonization. But we failed to rectify the damage after the Hindus overwhelmingly got de-facto power in 1947. For this transfer of power, we sacrificed one quarter of Akhand Hindustan territory to settle those Muslims who could not bear to live or adjust with the Hindu majority.

That is, by a failure to usher a renaissance after 1947, India lost her opportunity to cleanse the accumulated dirt and unwanted baggage of the past. The nation missed a chance to demolish the birth-based caste system, as Ambedkar had wanted to do. The battering that the concept of Hindu unity and Indian identity has taken at the hands of Nehruvian secularists since 1947, has led to the present social malaise. Thus, even though Hindus constitute more than 80 per cent of the population in India, they have not been able to understand their roots in, and obligations to, the nation in a pluralistic Hindustani democracy.

Today the sacrilege of Hindu concepts and hoary institutions, is being carried out *not with* the crude brutality of a Ghazni, or the savagery of Robert Clive, but with the sophistication of the constitutional instruments of law. The desecration of Hindu icons, for example the recent criminal cases filed against the Kanchi Kamakoti Mutt and against Swami Ramdev, is being made to look legal, thereby completely confusing the Hindu people, and thus making them unable to recognize the danger, or to realize that Hindus have to unite against the threats to their legacy. *We Hindus are under siege today, and we do not know it!!* That is, what is truly alarming is that Hindu society could be dismembered today without much protest since we have been lulled into cmplacency or have lost the capacity to think collectively as Hindus.

To resist this siege we first need Hindu unity. The actual numbers [of those claiming to be adherents to Hinduism] does not matter in today's information society. It is the durability and clarity of the Hindu mindset of those who unite that matters in the forging of an instrument to fight this creeping danger.

For example, recently we had a near disaster in Ayodhya: Pakistan—trained foreign terrorists slipped into India and traveled to Ayodhya to blow up the Ram Mandir. Their attempt was foiled by courageous policemen. But did the representative government of 870 million Hindus of India react in a meaningful way—that is did it retaliate to deter such attacks in future? Did anyone raise it in Parliament and demand deterrent retaliation? On the contrary, the Prime Minister assured Pakistan that peace talks will not be affected by such acts. But what retaliation was there to be for the sponsors of those terrorists who dared to think of blowing up Sri Ram's birth place? No wonder, terrorists have continued to target and disrupt India, and Hindus are their focus.

Thus today Hindus are being systematically prepared for psychological enslavement and conceptual capture. Indians are being subtly brain-washed. Hindus are being lulled, while Muslims and Christians are being subject to relentless propaganda that they are different, and are citizens of India as would be a shareholder in a company run for profit.

Hindus cannot fight this unless first what has to be confronted is identified. We cannot effectively respond unless we understand the nature and complexity of the challenge. What makes the task of defending Hinduism much more difficult today is that the oppressors are not obvious marauding entities as were Ghazni, Ghori, or Clive. The means of communications and the supply of funds in the hands of our enemies are multiples of that available in the past, for camouflaging their evil purposes.

My contention here is that Hindus today are facing a four dimensional siege and this siege is pernicious, clandestine, deceptive and sophisticated. It requires an enlightened Hindu unity to combat such threats and get the siege lifted. First, we have to begin by first understanding the content and scope of the siege before we Hindus can unite to battle it. These four dimensions are:

1. The clandestine defamation of Hindu symbols and institutions

The effect of this is to make Hindus lose their self-esteem by disparaging their tradition,—which also had been the strategy of British imperialists for the conquest of India. Speaking in the British Parliament, Lord Macaulay said on February 2, 1835 the following:

> *"Such wealth I have seen in this country [India], such high moral values, people of such calibre, that I do not think we would ever conquer this country unless we break the very backbone of this nation, which [backbone] is her spiritual and cultural heritage. And therefore, I propose that we replace her old and ancient education system, her culture, for if the Indians think that all that is foreign and English is good and greater than their own, they will lose their self-esteem, their native self-culture and they will become what we want them, a truly dominated nation".*

That basic strategy of those who want to see a weak and pliant India remains. Only the tactics have changed. Now the target is the Hindu institutions and Hindu icons; and the route is not the creation of a comprador class to subdue the nation, but is the fostering of a psychological milieu to denigrate the heritage and to delink the Hindu from his past legacy thereby causing a loss of self-esteem and of pride in the nation's past. There are already many examples of this happening.

A false murder case was foisted on the Acharyas of the 2500 year old Kanchi Mutt. Most Hindus have watched it as spectators, and with nagging doubts about the truth, and in fact about the Acharyas themselves. The Supreme Court has however held that the case has "no worthwhile prima facie evidence..." [Court records: (2005) 2 Supreme Court Cases 13, para 12, page 20] and that the alleged confessions of other accused persons implicating the Acharyas "have very little evidentiary value" [para 10]. The case thus is without basis and is bogus because since then the Tamil Nadu police has failed to uncover any further or new evidence to sustain the case. That the apex Court has found the foisted case as without prima facie merit should itself have galvanized the people against the offending authorities. It has not, because Hindus lack the mindset and guidance to retaliate against the willful and disguised defamation of Hindu symbols and institutions. Instead like parrots, most Hindus mouth the phrase that "law must take its course". Where is the law in this? Nor did a single Muslim or Christian organization or their leaders condemn this atrocity, exposing secularism as a one-way obligation of Hindus.

That the obvious perpetrator of this blasphemous atrocity on a hoary institution of the Hindus, was the head of the Tamil Nadu state government, one who also claims to be a good Hindu because she regularly visits temples, has only helped to further confound the already confused Hindu mind from responding.

That this atrocity could not have been heaped on the Mutt without the aid and abetment, or even the instigation of the power behind the throne in Delhi, a devout foreign-born Catholic, has not even evoked any anger amongst the Hindus.

Instead the majority of Hindus have been just passive or at most satisfied with discussing gossip *i.e.*, whether there was some land dispute of the Mutt with the government that triggered it or a money angle row with a politician in power to motivate the misuse of state machinery, to frame a Shankaracharya on a murder charge! It is incredible that in a nation of more than 80 per cent Hindus, the democratically elected state government dared to foist a bogus case on a Shankaracharya, and without a spontaneous uproar and mass protest by Hindus. That this atrocity could be the beginning of further assault on the foundation of the Hindu religion to defame and discredit it, should have jolted the Hindus into a fierce protest.

Otherwise, the current Hindu apathy will encourage further assault on Hindu institutions. It is already happening and there is no time to lose. In July 2005, an uncouth official of the Tamil Nadu Government's HR&CE Ministry blocked the Kanchi Shankaracharyas from entering the holy Shiva temple in Rameshwaram because, the official said, the acharyas had criminal cases pending against them. Leave aside the fact that anyone is presumed to be innocent until proved guilty beyond a reasonable doubt, or that Ms. Jayalalithaa, the CM herself then is clothed from head to foot in criminal cases, what is significant is the audacity of an official in a 80% plus Hindu populated country to block a Shankaracharya from performing his God-ordained puja duties. His HR&CE counterpart in Andhra, at Tirumala, has pontificated recently that the Tirumala hills, except a small portion, do not belong to Lord Venkateswara, making a mockery of *agama shastras*. Obviously, no penalty attaches to sneering at Hindu beliefs.

On the other hand, every facility is made available to minority wishes. The state government of Karnataka for example, soon after the Kanchi Acharya's arrest, blatantly patronized the congregation of a certain Benny Hinn who is under US Internal Revenue Service investigation. Even US Christian organizations, such as the Trinity Foundation, have exposed this man as a fake. Yet in the admiring presence of the Karnataka Chief Minister, with his Ministers in tow, and Central Government Ministers, Benny Hinn was allowed to usurp the Bangalore Air Force campus and hold a rally to denounce Hindu concepts and demonstrate his "cure" of some allegedly hopelessly and terminally ill or handicapped persons just by placing his hand, in the name of Jesus, on their heads. Bangalore police officers later told the media that the whole exercise was a fraud since the "ailing persons were trucked in from Erode in Tamil Nadu a week earlier and trained to fake the ailments and the cry of being cured on stage." Of course they were well paid for this deception. Such obscurantism was however extolled by the Congress Party leaders, while mouthing secularism. Benny Hinn in the end publicly boasted that a "friend of Sonia Gandhi" had helped to clear the way to make the Bangalore event possible.

The existence of a nexus had thus tumbled out. Taking a cue, other foreign Christian missionaries in trouble with the law, such as Mr. Ron Watts, made a pilgrimage to Delhi and received relief from law enforcers on the same patronage.

These visiting fraud Christian missionaries have the intellectual endorsement for proselytizing activities from well established Christian leaders. Cardinal Joseph Ratzinger, now Pope Benedict, an acknowledged leader of Catholics world over, had released a Vatican document in 1997 titled *Dominus Jesus,* in which both Hinduism and it's sister religion Buddhism have been denounced. While releasing the document, the Pope has been quoted as saying that Hinduism offers "false hope" and is "morally cruel" since it is based on the concept of reincarnation that resembles "a continuous circle of hell". He denounced Buddhism as "auto erotic spirituality". US based evangelist Pat Robertson has declared that to liberate Hindus from their bondage, "missionaries will seek to convert 100 million Hindus" over the next few years.

For achieving this goal, even tainted money is welcome for any missionary from abroad. Thus, Mother Teresa whose proselytizing activities were perhaps the most camouflaged of all foreign missionaries in India, once wrote to a US Court judge, Judge Ito in

Los Angeles asking that he not hold guilty one of her contributors by name Charles H. Keating Jr. (who was on trial in Judge Ito's court for criminally defrauding nominees of 17,000 persons of $ 252 million [about Rs. 1200 crores]). Mother Teresa' plea to the Judge was that since Mr. Keating had donated millions of dollars to her Missionaries of Charity, he should be let off and not be found guilty or even be prosecuted!

The Judge asked the Deputy District Attorney [equivalent of assistant public prosecutor in India] to reply to Mother Teresa's letter. Mr. Paul Turley wrote back to her giving the details of the case [by then Mr. Keating had been found guilty and convicted of fraud]. Mr. Turley in his letter advised Mother Teresa as follows: "Ask yourself what Jesus would do if he were given the fruits of a crime? I submit that Jesus would promptly and unhesitatingly have returned the stolen property to the rightful owners. You should do the same. Do not keep the money". Mother Teresa did not in fact hesitate at all. She kept the ill gotten money and ignored the advice!

According to the Ministry of Home Affairs, in 2002-03 private bodies with FCRA permission had received Rs. 5046 crores as contribution from abroad. In 2005-06 insiders have estimated these contributions at Rs. 7500 crores, of which two-thirds was going to Christian missionary organizations. This hefty sum has been used essentially for conversion and to defame Hinduism. Without defamation of Hinduism, conversion is not easy for these missionaries.

Another route to defame Hinduism is the textbook portrayal of Hindu society. Already Swami Ramakrishna Parmahans has been described in disparaging terms in government prescribed text books. Traitor Raja Jai Chand has been described as a hero, and Prithviraj as a coward! Since English language provides a fast track channel to India from abroad for propagation of ideas, books rubbishing Hindu gods and goddesses, sanyasis, and other icons are being published abroad and imported for use in India's public schools. Lord Ganesha has repeatedly been portrayed in most hurtful terms. Shiva linga has been ridiculed.

2. Demographic Restructuring of Indian Society

People of India who declare in the Census that they are adherents of religions born on Indian soil, that is Hindus, Sikhs, Buddhists, and Jains constituted 84.21% of the total Indian population in 2001. In 1941 the proportion, adjusted for Partition, was 84.44%. This figure hides the fact that Hindus resident in undivided Pakistan have migrated to post-Partition India which is why the share of Hindus and co-religionists have barely reduced since 1941. In the area called Bangladesh, Hindus were 30% in 1941. In 2001 they are less than 8%. In Pakistan of today. Hindus were 20% in 1941, and less than 2% in 2001. Such ethnic cleansing has not been noticed by anybody. If the figures are adjusted for such migration, then in the five decades 1951-2001, Hindus have lost more than 3 per cent points in share of Indian population, while Muslims have increased their share by about 3%. What is even more significant is that Hindus have lost 12% points since 1881, and the loss in share has begun to accelerate since 1971 partly due to illegal migration from Bangladesh.

The lack of Hindu unity and the determined bloc voting in elections by Muslims and Christians, has created a significantly large leverage for these two religious communities in economic, social and foreign policy making. Although the need for a uniform civil code is enshrined as a directive principle of state policy in the Constitution, it is taboo to demand it because of this leverage. Politicians fearing backlash anger of Christian and Muslim preachers are also unable to defend the need for continuation of a law to ban religious conversions that occur through inducements and coercion. In the case of Tamil Nadu, in 2004 the US Consul General in Chennai called on the Chief Minister to seek reversal of such a statute [www.state.gov/g/drl/rls/irf/2004/35516.htm]. He had been empowered to raise this issue by a 1998 Act of the US Congress on religious freedom. Incidentally, the AIADMK was administered a blistering defeat in the 2004 Parliament elections by a total consolidation of Muslim and Christian votes against the party because it's government had got passed such a law. After the elections, a humbled Chief Minister Ms. Jayalalithaa, capitulated and got the law annulled. I had put the US administration to test by asking the Ambassador in New Delhi if the US would demonstrate its even-handedness by asking the Tamil Nadu Chief Minister whether she will withdraw all the bogus cases foisted on the Kanchi acharyas on the same principles. The reply I got was that the Acharyas face criminal charges and hence the US will not intervene even if these charges are false.

The continued rise in the share of Muslims and Christians in the total population, is a threat to the Hindu foundation of the Nation. And we have to find ways and means to meet this threat. Kerala is a state where the Hindu population has declined from 69% in 1901: a hundred years later, in 2001, the share has fallen to 56%. Muslims are now 25% and Christians 19%. But the Hindu share in agricultural activities has fallen to 24%, while for Christians the share has risen to 40%. For Muslims it is 33%. In commerce and industry too, the same proportions exist, while as to employment in foreign companies, the Hindu share is just 19%, Muslims 49.5% and Christians 31.5%.

In the fertile districts of Western UP, from Rampur to Saharanpur, Muslims, due to a much higher population growth rate, are now 40% of the population. Six of the 14 districts of Assam in the northeast are already Muslim majority, and by 2031, all fourteen will be Muslim majority if present trends of differential population growth rate and illegal migration from Bangladesh continue.

In northeast India, minus Assam, 45.5% of the population is already Christian. Every one of the seven sister states has a galloping

Christian population. Arunachal which had zero Christian population in 1971, now has over 7%.

These two communities today fiercely safeguard their control of institutions spawned on public money besides receiving funds from abroad. Take for example the educational institutions. Jamia Millia Islamia University has been recognized as a central university with liberal government grants; but 88% of the faculty is Muslim. American College Madurai's faculty is 66% Christian. It's junior faculty is 95% Christian. Union Christian college at Aluva, Kerala has 83% Christian faculty. There are no exceptions. All institutions run by Muslims and Christians have grossly disproportionate share of their co-religionists. It is only recently that Allahabad High Court struck down as unconstitutional, the central university, the Aligarh Muslim University (AMU), reserving more than 50 percent of the admissions and faculty positions for Muslims. The Hindu tax payers' money was used all these decades to fund the AMU!

Thus, differential application of family planning, non-uniform civil code, illegal migration, and induced religious conversion have together created a serious looming crisis for the Hindu foundation of the nation. We see what Muslim majority will mean to Hindus when we look at the situation in Kashmir. We can learn from how Muslim majority will treat minorities or even women of Muslim faith when we look around the world and study Islamic nations. This is because *Muslims* believe the world is bifurcated as Darul Islam (where Muslims are in a majority and the rulers), and Darul Harab (in which Muslims are in a minority and are entitled by the Koran and Shariat, by hook or crook to transform these countries to Muslim ruled and/or Muslim majority). At present India is viewed as Darul Harab, and unless the Hindu majority compels or persuades the Muslim minority to enter into a contract to live in peace, whence India becomes Darul Ahad, the Muslim population will always play host to fanatics bent upon creating upheaval in India. That is why I am emphasizing that Muslims in

India must declare that their origin and ancestors are Hindus, and that Hindustan is their *matrubhoomi* and *karmabhoomi*. Christians too have their view of the world as divided between *heathens* (who have to be 'saved' by conversion) and followers of Jesus Christ. Now with the publication of Dan Brown's *Da Vinci Code* and its revelations about the Opus Dei organization, Hindus have to go on high alert about Christian missionaries from abroad. Moreover, patriots concerned with the safeguarding of the Hindu foundation of the nation have to take note that conversion to Christian faith has been put on a war footing by entrepreneurs. In Dallas, Texas USA, the Global Pastors Network [GPN] held a conference and resolved that over the next fifteen years, the organization will support financially worldwide the construction of five million churches and conversion of one billion persons to Christianity. According to the Evangelist Pat Robertson, for India alone the target is 100 million persons. *Hence, Hindus are facing a terrible pincer; Islamic fast population growth and illegal migration, in conjunction with Christian money–induced conversion activities.*

Hence, Hindus must hang together or ultimately they will hang separately. This is no inflamed psychosis. Not long ago, despite being the overwhelming majority, Hindus had to pay discriminatory taxes to the Muslim and Christian emperors who were ruling India. Lack of unity was the reason, and not poverty. In fact, when the onslaught and enslavement took place, India was the richest country in the world. Within 150 years thereafter, we were reduced to nearly the poorest in the world. Now if the demographic restructuring described herein goes on unchecked, then the danger becomes manifold.

3. The Rise of Terrorism Directed at Hindus

If one were to study the terrorism in Kashmir and Manipur, it is apparent that Hindus have been the special target. The driving away of the Hindu population from the Kashmir valley by the targeted terrorism of Islamic Jihadis, is the single biggest human rights atrocity since Nazi Germany perpetrated its pogroms against the Jews. Yet, it has hardly received notice in international fora. Why? In Bangladesh, by deliberate targeted ethnic cleansing, Islamic fanatics aided and abetted by their government, have caused the Hindu population to decline from 30 per cent to less than 8 percent of the total population [see *Hindus in Bangladesh, Pakistan and India's State of Jammu & Kashmir: A Survey of Human Rights*, Jun 17, 2005, www.hinduamericanfoundation.org], and yet there is no outcry. Why? This is because Hindus lack the mindset to retaliate against atrocities against Hindus. When in 1949, anti Hindu riots took place in East Pakistan, Sardar Patel had declared that if the government there could not control it, then India was quite capable of putting it down for them. Soon after the riots stopped. Terrorist attacks against India (and Hindus and their institutions in particular) thus are growing because we seem today incapable of retaliating in a manner that deters future attacks.

In its report entitled "A Chronology of International Terrorism for 2004" the well known *National Counter-terrorism Center,* a US government body, states that: "India suffered more significant acts of terrorism than any other country in 2004":—a damning comment. India is suffering on an average about 25 incidents of terrorism a month. India's Home Ministry in it's 2004-05 Annual Report to Parliament acknowledges that 29 of the 35 states and union territories are affected by terrorism. Moreover, all India's neighbours have become hot-beds for anti-Indian terrorists training.

Because of Hindu disunity and its lack of the mindset to deter retaliation, terrorists have become encouraged. In 1989, the Indian government released five dreaded terrorists to get back Rubaiyya, the kidnapped daughter of the then Home Minister. Kashmir terrorists got a huge boost by this capitulation. When an Indian Airlines plane with 239 passengers was hijacked to Kandahar,

Afghanistan, the government again capitulated and released three of the most dangerous terrorists. Today three of the most murderous terrorist organizations in Kashmir are directed by these three freed terrorists. Then there is the case of the LTTE which murdered Rajiv Gandhi. We have made no effort to apprehend the leader of the LTTE who had ordered the assassination. On the contrary, those MPs [of PMK, MDMK, and DMK] who publicly praise that leader and hold the assassination as justified, have become Union Ministers in a government formed by a coalition led by the widow of Rajiv Gandhi!

Terrorism cannot be fought by appeasement. But that precisely is what the government is doing. Tragically, innocent Hindus have invariably been the victims of this capitulation. To combat terrorism, there has to be a determination never to negotiate a settlement with terrorists. Citizens of a country have to be educated that there will be hazards when faced with acts of terrorism, but that the goal of the government will always have to be to hunt down the terrorists and fix them. Only under such a zero tolerance policy towards terrorism, will the ultimate good emerge. For example, in the Indian Airlines hijack case, in order not to risk the lives of 239 passengers, the government released Mohammed Azhar from jail. But Azhar went to Pakistan after his release and formed the Jaish-e-Mohammed which has since then killed nearly a thousand innocent Hindus and is still continuing to do so. How then has the Nation gained by the Kandahar capitulation?

Hence the Hindus of India, and other Indians too should treat the fight against terrorism, as a *dharamayudh* as a fight to the finish and a religious duty not to negotiate or compromise with, or capitulate to terrorists. The government must also safeguard the nation by adopting a policy of "hot pursuit" of terrorists by chasing them to their sanctuaries, no matter in which country such sanctuaries are located.

4. The Erosion of Moral Authority of Governance

The well known organization *Transparency International* has graded about 140 countries according to the corruption levels from the least to the most. India appears near the bottom of the list as among the most corrupt. Recently *The Mitrokhin Archieves II* has been published wherein KGB documents have been relied on to conclude that shamefully "India was on sale for KGB bribes". If India is one of the most corrupt countries today and purchasable, it is because the core Hindu values of simplicity, sacrifice and abstinence have been systematically downgraded over the years. Wealth obtained by any means has become the criterion for social status. There was a time in India when persons of learning and simplicity enjoyed the moral authority in society to make even kings bow before them. Not long ago, Mahatma Gandhi and later Jayaprakash Narayan, without holding office were here exercising the same moral authority over political leaders. In a very short period, that Hindu value system has evaporated. India is fast becoming a banana republic in which everything, person or policy is available to anyone for a price. The proposal, now implemented in some states, to have reservation in government employment for Muslims and "Dalit" Christians is one such sell-out. Reservation quotas are strictly for those whom a degenerated Hindu society had suppressed or had isolated from the mainstream. But those who were ruling classes in our nation, such as Muslims and Christians, (and that too for a total of a thousand years), cannot claim this facility. But some political parties, in reckless disregard of equity and history, have sold out the national interest for bloc votes: by advocating for such a reservation proposal. In such a situation the Nation's independence and sovereignity slides into danger of being subverted and then rendered impotent. This has happened before in our history,—not when the nation was poor but when it was one of the richest countries in the world. India then was ahead in science, mathematics, art and architecture. And yet because the moral fibre weakened, all was lost. We had to struggle hard to recover our freedom. But by the time we did, we had lost all our wealth and dropped near to the bottom of the list of countries, listed according to level of poverty.

In this time of creeping darkness in our society, there are still venerated souls who draw crowds of people, who come at their own expense to hear such evolved souls and follow them. These are our dharmacharyas, many of whom should constitute a Hindu Dharma Acharya Sabha. Just as Rishi Vishwamitra picked his archers and hunters to put an end to *asuras* and *rakshasas*, in the same way I urge and implore this Sabha to pick a political instrument to cleanse the body politic of the nation. It cannot be done without Hindu unity in our democracy, and hence formulating a code of ethics and moral principles is essential for creating a meaningful and purposeful Hindu unity. The nation looks to all dharma acharyas, for guidance in this hour of need.

But first and foremost is the need for the undiluted unity of Hindus, a unity based on a mindset that is nurtured and fostered on the fundamentals of a renaissance. Only then can Hindus meet the challenge of Christian missionaries and Islamic fundamentalists. I can do no better here than quote Swami Dayananda Saraswati of Arsha Vidya Gurukulam:

> *"Faced with militant missionaries, Hinduism has to show that its plurality and all-encompassing acceptance are not signs of disparateness or disunity. For that, a collective voice is needed."*

Non-Hindus can join to create a Hindustani unity, but first they must agree to adhere to the minimum requirement: that they recognize and accept that their cultural legacy is Hindu, or that they revere their Hindu origins, that they are as equal before law as any other but no more, and that they will make sacrifices to defend their Hindu legacy just as any good Hindu would his own. In turn then the Hindu will defend such non-Hindus as they have the Parsis and Jews, and accept them as the Hindustani *pariwar*.

India can be only for those who swear that Bharatvarsh or Hindustan is their *matrubhoomi* and *karmabhoomi*. Since the task to defeat the nefarious forces ranged today against Hindu Society is not going to be easy, we cannot therefore trust those in our midst whose commitment to the motherland is ambivalent or *ad hoc or those who feel no kinship to the Hindu past of the nation*. We partitioned a quarter of Hindustan to accomodate those Muslims who could not live with us Hindus in a democratic framework of equality and fraternity. Hence now only those are true children of Bharatmata who accept that India is their *matrubhoomi* and *karmabhoomi;* and only these are welcome in naveen (new) Hindustan to be created out of a renaissance.

As Swami Vivekananda said to Hindus: "Arise, Awake and Go Forth as Proud Hindus". But what does being a proud Hindu entail? The core of what it entails can be found by gleaning the writings of our sages and interpreting it in the modern context. I have tried summarizing the distilled wisdom in the following axioms or fundamentals of Hindu Unity that also define the Hindu mindset:

First, a Hindu, and those others who are proud of their Hindu past and origins, *must know the correct history of India:* that history which records that Hindus have always been, and are one; that caste is not birth-based and nor immutable; that India is a continuum; sanatana; that ancient Hindus and their descendents have always lived in this area from the Himalayas to the Indian Ocean, an area called Akhand Hindustan, and that they did not come from outside; (rather that Hindus went from India, abroad to spread knowledge) and that there is not truth in the Aryan-Dravidian race theory.

Second, Hindus believe that all religions equally lead to God, but *not that* all religions are equal in the richness of their theological content. Respecting all religions, Hindus must demand from others that such respect is a two-way obligation. That is, if Hindus are to defend the right of others to adhere to their own religion, then other religionists have to stand up for Hindus too. By this criterion, secular attitude as defined till date, has been a one-way obligation for Hindus. Hence Hindus must reject such a concept because of its implied appeasement. At the same time enlightened Hindus must defend and protect vigorously those non-Hindus, who accept that their ancestors and their culture are Hindu. A vibrant Bharatvarsh cannot be home to bigotry and obscurantism since that has never been Hindu tradition or history. But Muslims and Christians shall be part of the Hindustani parivar or family only if they accept this truth and revere it.

Third, Hindus must prefer to lose everything they possess rather than submit to tyranny or to terrorism. Today those in India who submit to terrorists and hijackers must be vehemently despised as anti-Hindu. They cannot be good Hindus merely because they are citizens of India. A good Hindu must have the mindset to stand up to tyranny and terrorism.

Fourth, the Hindu must have a mindset to retaliate when attacked. The retaliation must be massive enough to deter future attacks. If terrorists come from training camps in Pakistan, *Bangladesh* or Sri Lanka, India must seek to carpet bomb those training camps, no matter the consequences. Today's so-called self proclaimed "good" Hindus have failed to avenge or retaliate for the attacks on Parliament, Akshardham Mandir in Gujarat, the sanctum sanctorum in Ayodhya, and even a former Prime Minister's [Rajiv Gandhi's] assassination. On the other hand those who defend these assassins and praise the terrorist organizations behind them, are Central Government Ministers today.

Fifth, all Hindus to qualify as true Hindus must make effort to learn Sanskrit and the Devanagari script in addition to their own mother tongue; and must pledge that one day in the future, Sanskrit will be India's link language since all the main Indian languages already have large percentages of their vocabulary in common with Sanskrit.

These five fundamentals constitute the concept of virat Hindu unity, a bonding that Hindus need in order to be in position to confront the challenge that Hindu civilization is facing from Islamic terrorists and fraudulent Christian missionaries from abroad, who are also aided and abetted by confused Hindus who have not grasped these fundamentals. Without such a *virat* Hindu unity and its implied mindset, we will be unable to nullify and root out the subversion and erosion that today undermine, the Hindu foundation of India. This foundation is what makes India distinctive in the world; and hence we must safeguard this legacy with all the might and moral fibre that we can muster. This mindset must be implemented by a clear vision on economic strategy, national security, and the national language medium for informed communication. The Hindu mindset and associated policies consistent with that mindset would lead Hindus out of the siege. That is why an Agenda is essential. In this we can get great moral support from Hindus resident abroad because of their sheer commitment to the Motherland. Free from economic constraints, aching for an identity, and well educated, I have seen them organize effectively to challenge the attempts to slander Hindu religious symbols and icons. Overseas Hindustanis have contributed during our Freedom Struggle, during the Emergency, and in enabling our acharyas to spread the message of the Hindu religion abroad. This has been done without demeaning other religions.

Since in a democracy the battle is in fighting elections, we therefore must resolve to foster a Hindu consciousness that leads to a cohesive vigorous Hindu unity and mindset, so that the Hindustani voter will cast his ballot only for those candidates in an election who will be loyal to a Hindu Agenda drawn up by the Dharamacharyas. We therefore, need an Acharya Sabha, acknowledged by the moral majority in India as an *informal* third chamber to the Lok Sabha and Rajya Sabha.

2.

The First Fundamental:
The Concept of India a Hindustan

A genuine Hindu awakening cannot be directed against any other community. A renaissance which aims at self-purification and renewal is by definition liberal. Bigots and compradors are forever afraid of liberals. The fundamental freedoms which such a renaissance affords to the individual will frighten any reactionary.

In case of the Muslims, the basic fear of a renaissance is that thereby even if it is given only an indirect chance, Hinduism will assimilate the Muslim into the Hindu fold. This fear is understandable. Everyone knows how Hinduism accommodated and then absorbed within its framework Buddhism, Jainism, Sikhism and now Zoroastrianism. However, such a parallel cannot be drawn for Islam. Buddha, Mahavir and Guru Nanak were Hindus who founded their religious schools in order to preach a more enlightened and liberated version of what we later accepted as within the basic structure of Hinduism. Zoroaster may have gone from Vahika Prant of India to Persia. The Zend Avesta, the scripture of Zoroastrianism is very close in theology to Hinduism. In particular, in essence therefore, none of these holy men ceased to be Hindu-like since the *sanctum sanctorum* of their theology is cloned Hindu.

Who is then a Hindu? From what I have been able to learn, a person—if that person wants to be called a Hindu—is one if he believes in the following nine points that constitute the core of Hindu theological beliefs. Thus such a person is deemed to be a Hindu if he:

1. Believes in one, all-pervasive Supreme being who is both Immanent and transcendent, both Creator and Unmanifest Reality.
2. Believes that the universe undergoes endless cycles of creation, preservation and dissolution.
3. Believes that all souls are evolving towards union with God and will ultimately find *moksha*, spiritual knowledge and liberation from the cycle of rebirth. Not a single soul will be eternally deprived of this destiny.
4. Believes in *karma*, one law of cause and effect by which each individual creates his own destiny by his thoughts, words and deeds.
5. Believes that the soul reincarnates, evolving through many births until all *karmas* have been resolved.
6. Believes that divine beings exist in unseen worlds and that temple worship, rituals and sacraments as well as personal devotion can create a communion with these *devtas* and Gods in one's lifetime.
7. Believes that a spiritually awakened Master or Sat Guru is helpful to know the Transcendent Absolute, as are personal discipline, good conduct, purification, self-inquiry, and meditation.
8. Believes that all life is sacred and to be loved and revered, and believes too in the practice of *ahimsa* or non-violence.
9. Believes that no particular religion teaches the *only* way to salvation above all others, but that all genuine religious paths are facets of God's Pure Love and Light, deserving tolerance and understanding.

Shorn of the frills and fossilisation, this ancient religion, at the core believes that anyone who accepts these nine points is eligible to be a Hindu; but in the final analysis, that person must willingly want to be called Hindu. Clearly, Muslims, Christians and Jews cannot accept points 3, 6 and 9. For them there is only God Whom one can meet only after death (not in one's own lifetime) and then be consigned by Him to Heaven or Hell permanently. There is no question of re-incarnation.

Therefore the Muslims' fear of religious assimilation is quite unfounded, unless the fundamentalists apprehend that exposure to the quintessence of Hindu beliefs may weaken their hold on the Muslim community or might even lead followers of the Faith to question some of their own precepts. It is significant that in the Muslim ghettos or *Mohallas, the Mullahs* argued against the Supreme Court's decision in the Shah Bano case not on the merits of it, but on the ground that it represented the first step of "devious" Hindus to undermine Islam. If the Muslims did not protest, the *Mullahs* warned, then more subversion of the Faith would follow.

Why should the burden of national renaissance be on the shoulders of Hindus? Hindus are more than 80 per cent of India. For them, this is their only country and the land of the birth of their religion. The Vedas, Avatars, Gurus all are from this country. India is the land where Hindus live and in the eyes of the world, India has a Hindu cultural identity. Therefore, if Hindus take the initiative for self-purification and a renaissance, the dynamics of change will induce other religious minorities to willingly follow, without being coerced to do so, since it is after all their legacy as well. That is why renaming India as Hindustan would give that necessary focus to our country. The English world "India" is an adaptation from the Greek "Indi", which in turn came from the ancient Iranians calling our land "Hindu" to represent the areas beyond the Sindhu. All those who came to India from time immemorial (from Fa Hsien, to Vasco da Gama, to traders, scholars, plunderers, tyrants and even the early imperialists) have called this land Hindustan. In colloquial speech, Muslims, and other minorities even today call India as Hindustan. Iqbal's heart-warming poem cum lyric "Sare Jahan se Achha..." ends with Hindustan.

No hardline Muslim leader therefore can think such a renaming objectionable. The word Hindustan is also a *Sandhi* of two words – Himalayas (Hi) and Indu Sagar (Indu), and secular in construction. There is no connotation of a Hindu theocratic state in the term Hindustan, while *Hindu Rashtra* may have been given such a connotation by it's critics. Therefore, I am at a loss to understand why at the time of framing our Constitution, we chose to begin the Preamble with the words "India that is Bharat", instead of "India that is Hindustan". *Paradoxically, Bharat has a religious connotation, while Hindustan does not.* One has to read the *Vishnu Purana* to recognize that.

Hindustan does not mean that the land belongs to the Hindus. Even on that score a citizen has a claim to Hindustan by birth. In fact, whoever has lived in India, has had forefathers who were Hindus. Even the Parsis and Jews have intermarried with Hindus. The term 'Hindustan' is thus appropriate to describe India because as K.M. Panikkar once noted: "In essence, therefore, the history of Indian effort towards the building up and maintenance of a specially Indian civilization has to be the history of the Hindu mind and its achievements". Panikkar argues that the Islamic contribution is not specially traced to India but is a part of a world culture to which Indian Muslims belong. To the extent it is Indian, as in the case of Moghul painting or Indo-Saracenic architecture, the differentiating characteristic is largely Hindu that worked out in the interaction. Just as the Ganga river is known as Ganga despite so many rivers merging into it along its journey to the sea, India's historical mainstream is Hindu despite the contribution to it by Islam and Christianity.

In other words, we reject the notion of India as a multinational state as advocated by the communists. Instead India, that is Hindustan, has an organic cultural core which is Hindu in character. But in the reigns of Hindu Kings this Hindustan has been secular in the enlightened sense discussed in the next Chapter.

The Hindu foundation of modern India is also why India has been, (and is even today), referred to in India and abroad as Hindustan. Hindustan, as stated above is defined as a nation of Hindus and those who accept that their ancestors are Hindus. The concept also includes refugee minorities who accept the core values of the Hindu culture and are therefore recognized as a part of the Hindustan nation. Thus, when the Dwarka Mutt Shankaracharya gave the Parsi refugees landing in Sanjaan [on the Gujarat coast] a five point requirement for settling in the country, they readily accepted and have not deviated from it even today. These five points were: giving up the Persian language and adopting Gujarati; wearing Indian clothes instead of Persian; treating the cow as sacred; reciting some select Sanskrit slokas in their marriage ceremony; and laying down weapons. Despite being the smallest minority, (with a disproportionate share in offices of power and national wealth), and perhaps also the wealthiest community, there is and has been no tension or conflict between Hindus and Parsis.

Parsis and Jews do not threaten the Hindu character of the nation. They do not seek to proselytize or convert Hindus by monetary or heavenly inducements or by obscurantist preachings such as claiming to cure persons who convert simply by the might of the Bible. In contrast the preachings of the religious leaders of Islam and Christianity in India, altogether for a thousand years, had targeted Hindus and sought religious conversions to their faiths by creating deprivation and loss of self esteem, through the abuse of the power of the State against Hindus. They were not even subtle about it. For example, in 1545, King John III of Portugal gave a command to the then Governor of Goa that neither public nor private 'idols' of Hindu heathens should be tolerated in Goa and that severe punishment must be meted out to those who persist in keeping them. Thereafter, a terrible inquisition followed during which Hindus were killed and brutalized, and their temples razed to the ground. We must not forget that despite this, only a minority of Hindus converted to Christianity. No other religious community other than Hindus suffered such prolonged and atrocious persecution and survived as a religion of a vast majority on their own soil. Let us not forget this defiance in our past.

Today, Hindus, despite being in defacto power and in the organs of the state, are victims of that same targeting, but of course in a very subtle and sophisticated manner. In furthering the objective of this targeting, Islam and Christianity, more so the latter, have been able to leverage the influence of prominent Hindus themselves, who wittingly (for money), or unwittingly (because of a programmed mindset of being defensive about being a Hindu and thereby being ready to ape the West) are tools of this targeting.

What is the nature and scope of this targeting, and is there a way for us to end it by conciliation with Christians and Muslims? In other words, can we seek to end religious conversion in India today by the ancient Hindu way of *shashtrathas* as Hindu saints did—as for example Adi Sankara did with Buddhism & Uttara Mimamsa theologies and Azhwars and Nayanars saints in the south did with Jainism? Will indeed Christians and Muslims recognize the sanctity of shashtratas?

There is a serious problem here. An interesting study of *Sarah Claerhout and Jakob De Roover* titled: "The Question of Conversion in India" [*Economic and Political Weekly, July 9, 2005*] concludes, that Hindus and Christians have fundamentally different and mutually exclusive concepts of religion and thus also in their approaches to the question of conversion. Hence, say the authors, for Hindus and Christians to dialogue on conversion would be fruitless because they will have "great difficulties making sense of each other's statements and arguments". This is because Hindus do not consider any religion as wholly false, and because as Gandhiji put it, all religions have some errors in them. Since according to the Hindu, all religions lead to God, hence there is no need for forcing a conversion. The Christian [and Muslim] thinks otherwise: that his is the only true religion, and it is God's work to convert heathens and *kafirs* to this only true religion.

I have thus come to the conclusion after much study and observing what has been, and is happening in India, that *there is a fundamental disconnect between the religious outlook of Hindus and the Christians and Muslims which makes it impossible for a fruitful debate and mutual understanding on the question of religious conversion.*

Therefore, either Hindus will have to capitulate on this question by permitting religious conversion in India, or in the alternative be united and assertive to ensure that laws are enacted and effectively enforced against religious conversion of Hindus. There is no third way.

I am persuaded that it is urgent now that Hindus be mobilized to assertively oppose any further conversion from Hinduism to any other non-Indian religion. There is no room for indifference here. This is because the status quo is damaging to the Hindu faith, since the Christian missionaries and Muslim mullahs are already fully at work, funds being no constraint, to convert Hindus. If conversions are not explicitly opposed, then Hindus are implicitly acquiescing in the atrocity.

Reflect on the past trends: In 1000 A.D., Muslims and Christians in undivided India were in negligible numbers. By 1400, they had become 3.5% of the sub-continent. In 1700, they rose to 11%, and by 1891 to 13%. By the time of Partition, they were 23%, and today in south Asia the Christian and Muslim population is 36%. What will it be in 2050 or 2150? This is an extraordinary rise, which has continued even after freedom from

British colonial rule. Defacto power in the hands of Hindu majority has not changed the attitude of the proselytizers; only their strategy has changed and become invisible for most Hindus. And those Hindus who have been in power in government have been soft on this issue entrapped by the lack of a Hindu mindset and by bloc voting by the Muslims and Christians.

Even the most secular Hindus should however worry about this demographic trend, because secularism is itself under threat if the Hindus lose their majority share in population. That is why even Gandhiji and Dr. Ambedkar [no Hindu fundamentalists but highly regarded secularists], during the Freedom Struggle had stoutly opposed religious conversions. In the Mahatma's interview given to The Hindu in 1931 [see Collected Works of Mahatma Gandhi. Vol XLV, p. 320] he stated:

> *"Every nation's religion is as good as another. Certainly India's religions are adequate for her people. We need no converting spiritually".*

Gandhiji went on to add that if foreign missionaries in independent India sought to convert by inducement such as by medical aid and in providing education, then he would ask them to withdraw from the country. Lest his remarks be treated as a misquote or off the cuff, Gandhiji later authored an article to reaffirm the same view in different language:

> *"India stands in no need of conversions from one faith to another"* Young India (April 23, 1931 issue)

When independent India debated the draft Constitution in the Constituent Assembly, enormous pressure was brought to bear within the Assembly and outside, to make the freedom to convert a fundamental right. Within the Assembly, the leader of Anglo-Indians, Mr. Frank Anthony stated that the right to convert to Christian faith was the "most fundamental of Christian rights" [Constituent Assembly Debates III; p. 489-90]. He and other Christian groups had wanted Article 25 to be so re-drafted as to make the right to carry on conversion activities as a fundamental right. But with the exception of a few, others did not agree. Dr. Ambedkar despite his own stated views against conversion as a right, was prevailed upon by Nehru to draft a hotch-potch Article 25*, which meant all things to all persons, which then was adopted by the Constituent Assembly.

However, soon after Independence, the pinch of induced conversion began to be felt, and some State Governments, notably Madhya Pradesh and Orissa enacted laws banning induced conversions. In 1977, a ruling Janata Party MP Om Prakash Tyagi brought forth a Private Member's Bill in the Lok Sabha to seek Parliamentary approval to get a law enacted to make induced conversions a national offence. Unfortunately, despite it having wide support, the Janata government did not last long enough to enact a law banning induced conversions.

In 1977, the Supreme Court clarified in a landmark judgement, (*Rev Stanislaus Vs State of Madhya Pradesh and Others*) that Article 25 however worded did not allow for the right to convert. Chief Justice A.N. Ray opined that "if a person purposely undertakes the conversion of another to his religion, that would impinge on the freedom of conscience guaranteed to all citizens of the country alike". Despite this clear ruling, governments that have come and gone have failed to translate the judgement into an explicit law. Since then the political play of secularism has continued to dilute the resolve of governments to stop induced conversions.

Now the freedom to convert has become of international concern. V.K. Shashikumar in an article titled: "Bush's Conversion Agenda for India", published in Tehelka in February 2004 states that a project code named JOSHUA projects I&II was formulated by

---

* Article 25(1), as finally enacted reads:

"25. **Freedom of conscience and free profession, practice and propagation of religion**—(1) subject to public order, morality and health and to the other provisions of this Part, all persons are equally entitled to freedom of conscience and the right freely to profess, practice and propagate religion."

US Evangelical groups to map the 1,52,786 post offices in India and codified by PIN codes, and then identify where and how conversion may be planned. Based on this project, a recent September 2005 conclave in Dallas, Texas targeted that 100 million converts from Hinduism should be achieved by 2020. Of course knowing the US scene as I do, there are other Christian groups in the US who are apprehensive that these Evangelical groups may end up giving Christianity a bad name, and they have been using the web blogs to expose these groups. One such concerned group, the Trinity Foundation had exposed Benny Hinn who had earlier been received almost as a State Guest in Bangalore to hold his fraud congregation to demonstrate his miracle cures. But India bears the brunt of the likes of Benny Hinn, and not Trinity Foundation. And when we speak of Christian missionaries we mean those whose mission is to proselytize. And of course it is an international effort and we need to make up our minds to have none of it.

As Chief minister of Tamil Nadu, Ms. Jayalalithaa brought into law a statute titled Tamil Nadu Prohibition of Forcible Conversion of Religion, but soon she had to beat a hasty retreat when the US Consul General based in Chennai met her and apprised her that the said statute violated US law on religious freedom. Ms. Jayalalithaa, though claiming to be a staunch Hindu, was devoid of courage and did not press the law. This was a sad capitulation for Indians in general and Tamils in particular. That is the mindset that we need to combat and alter.

I must make clear here however that *I do not oppose voluntary and unforced conversion to Hinduism of those presently of the Semitic religions, such as Christians and Muslims of India,* because all Indians, except Parsis and Jews are either Hindus or those whose ancestors were Hindus. Their becoming Hindus amounts to *re-conversion* and a return to the Hindu fold. For most Christians and Muslims in India, the conversion of their ancestors in the past was coerced openly, crudely, savagely, or subtly, but it was not voluntary. One has to read what happened to Guru Tegh Bahadur to imagine what else must have happened in the country to make Hindus to convert. Today, every Muslim and Christian in India is a living example of that despicable violence against the Hindus. We may try to understand what and why it had happened in the past, but we should not forget the lesson embedded in the brutally forced conversions that did take place. We should therefore all be thankful to Swami Dayananda Saraswati for his open letter to Pope John Paul II, during the latter's visit to New Delhi in 1999 to preach the Gospel. In that letter the Swamiji boldly stated:

> *"Religious conversion destroys centuries-old communities and incites communal violence.* It is violence, and it breeds violence" *[www.hindnet.org/conversion/pope99/].*

I am also not advocating that Hindus and the followers of other religions must confront each other, and not interact or dialogue on any issue. Far from it, I advocate vibrant debate and discussion on most religious issues, but not on those issues which will erode or undermine the Hindu foundation of India. On the question of religious conversion, it should now be treated as a closed chapter. Hindus true to their legacy will not permit it. Either, true Hindus will prevail, or India will be deformed and twisted; and ultimately, like Greece and Egypt, it will be transformed beyond recognition. India as the world has known it and admired it, would then be destroyed forever. Hence, instead Hindus must remain steadfast and carry the 'war' to the camps of the Christian missionaries and Muslims mullahs of India and make the Christians and Muslims see how they too can take pride in their great Hindu ancestry, and that they can be welcomed back to the Hindu fold. A Russian scholar, Alexander Zinoviev, of the Russian Academy of Sciences in Moscow, recently published an article in the Organiser, that was titled: "For India's Survival Hinduism has to Prevail". In it he states:

> *"....during the Renaissance, Western Europeans realized that they were successors of ancient Rome and Greece, and embraced their culture which*

for long centuries was being condemned by the Roman Catholic Church as "pagan" and "non-Christian", [hence] one day the Muslims on the Indian sub-continent will understand that they are inheritors of a great civilisation completely different from that of Arabs and the Middle East. This is a problem of education and knowledge"

Of course *before* we can motivate and persuade the Indian Christian and Muslims to accept that their ancestors are Hindus and that because of this fact they have the option of returning to Hinduism, *we Hindus have to set our house in order.* Over the centuries since Adi Shankaracharya, the Hindu religion has not undergone a renaissance. There have been valiant attempts, but these had been circumscribed by the political compulsions of the time foisted on us by invasions and imperialism. Often these attempts at renaissance had to be aborted due to these compulsions. In 1947 however we Hindus had an opportunity to usher a renaissance without compulsions; but the misfortune of a long tenure as Prime Minister of a self-confessed agnostic and the political culture imported from a God-less Communist Soviet Union thoroughly froze the distortions in Hindu religious practices. It is imperative therefore to create a new Hindu corporate awareness to confront these distortions frontally and remove them. Otherwise, the forces ranged against Hinduism today will succeed in their nefarious designs.

I am particularly concerned with the effect that the *varna vyavastha* [caste system] is having in promoting religious conversions. It gives a talking point to the enemies of Hinduism. It is not that other religions do not have a stratification based on origin of the individual. Dalit converts to Christianity for example learn the hard way about their low status in their new religion, and hence they are asking for reservation in jobs and education even after conversion! Of course, we should never agree to that because reservation is strictly a correction for the malfunction of the Hindu society in the past, and in fact reservations should have been confined to schedule castes and tribes only who have remained Hindus despite all the atrocities heaped on them for centuries.

Christians and Muslims have been ruling classes in India for a thousand years and hence they are certainly not deprived or discriminated against in any way. In that sense, persons belonging to the scheduled castes are more steadfast Hindus than those of other castes, for they have remained Hindus despite being deprived, humiliated and discriminated.

Moreover, I may add that I regard Dr. Ambedkar as the twentieth century intellectual who should be most admired by Hindu society for his profound perception of India's history which perception he has fortunately for all of us recorded in books and articles. Not only did he write like a Hindu patriot, but he can be regarded as a joint architect, with Mahatma Gandhi and Sardar Patel, of the geographical India of today. Had Dr. Ambedkar accepted the 1932 British imperialist offer for a separate electorate for scheduled castes, and had Gandhiji not staked his life against it, India would have been completely balkanized before the British left in 1947. That was the imperialist plot; and Dr. Ambedkar understood it and being a patriot he refused to oblige. It is a great tragedy for India that personal jealousies led to his sidelining in politics after Independence which ultimately frustrated him. It is not too late to express our veneration for him even now by a campaign to demolish what is left of the caste system.

We owe it to Dr. M.V. Nadkarni for a brilliant study titled: "Is Caste System Intrinsic to Hinduism?" [*Economic and Political Weekly*, November 8, 2003] wherein he has proved beyond anyone's reasonable doubt that "it is necessary to demolish the myth that caste system is an intrinsic part of Hinduism". Dr. Nadkarni further argues very convincingly that "the caste system emerged and survived due to totally different factors, which had nothing to do with Hindu religion". He concludes his study with a highly perceptive remark that the caste system "has collapsed today because all its functions have collapsed. It has lost whatever relevance, role, utility, and justification it may have had".

The caste system was never meant to create a Brahmin hegemony; nor was it conceived as birth-based. Brahmins were those venerated because they led a simple life and were devoted to education and religious theology. But to become a *Rishi* it was not necessary to be born of Brahmin parents. Valmiki, Veda Vyasa, Vishwamitra, and Kalidasa were not born in Brahmin families. Nor were Brahmins above the law. Ravana, a scholar of repute had to pay a heavy price for his abduction of Rama's wife. Caste identification instead was by *gunahs* [virtues], as Lord Krishna told Arjuna according to the Uttara Gita.

Nor do the recent researches on DNA of Indians show any racial differences amongst castes. So why tolerate a system which at the very least is obsolete and a stumbling block in the way of total Hindu unity? I urge all the *dharma gurus* and Acharyas, to find a way to campaign for the abolition of the caste system so that we may achieve a renaissance in Hinduism.

At this juncture in our history, nearly sixty years after securing freedom from successive oppressive regimes spread over a thousand years, empowered by a pluralistic democracy and on the verge of a major economic upsurge, Hindus are again finding themselves agonizing as to what the future holds for them as a religious community. Because of a greater readiness amongst Hindus to accept family planning and because elected governments over the years have failed to prevent illegal immigration of minorities from our neighbourhood, the Hindu share of the population is declining. More importantly, there are states of the Indian Union where Muslims and Christians are in majority, and Hindus are being denied their due in those states. In Kashmir, thousands and thousands of Hindus have been driven out in the despicably blatant religious cleansing. At this rate Hindus could become a minority within hundred years. In Tripura, Hindu activists are being murdered every day by Christian terrorists. In the south, a Shankaracharya Mutt has been defiled by the state government filing false and bogus murder cases against the a venerated Holy man. The Acharya was not permitted by a government official to perform his traditional pujas at the Rameshwaram temple because the Acharya had this bogus case pending against him!! Even the carrying of the *dand* by the junior Shankaracharya of Dwarka was opposed by the government run Indian Airlines, and the sant had to disembark from the plane he was sitting in. And all this is happening while Hindus are in power in the government.

Hence, Hindus need a new mindset, the composition of which is in detail in my speech on "Fundamentals of Hindu Unity and the Concept of Hindustan" delivered before the Second Hindu Dharma Acharya Sabha conference held in Mumbai on October 16-18, 2005. As I have said before, Hindus are under a siege, and they do not even know it. There is a war on, between "Om Shakti" and "Rome Bhakti" today through conversions.

Conversion activities are a symptom of the lack of a correct mindset among Hindus, and thus we must deal with this threat in that context. Most of all, Indians must be persuaded to accept the concept of India as Hindustan. The true Indian identity is that we are Hindus or our ancestors are Hindus, and native to the area from the Himalayas to the Hindu Sagar (Indian Ocean). That is the first fundamental of a Hindu mindset.

3.
The Second Fundamental:
Enlightened Secularism and Common Heritage

This brings me to the second Fundamental for Renaissance. That is secularism. Since there are a great many people living in India of different religious faiths, hence we need a concept of how people bond together and mutually accommodate their religious aspirations without conflict. Since a thousand years ago, India was a country of 100% Hindus, there is also a question on how to bond with our past since Islam and Christianity were imported into India. This bonding question has not been made clear to the Indian people, hence there is a great deal of confusion in the country on the meaning of secularism.

In the original meaning, secularism had merely meant separation of the temporal power from the dictates of the spiritual authority.

In Europe where the concept originated, the State was to be separate from the institutional authority or the Church. In a Hindu dominated country, there is no 'Church' for a Hindu religious authority, so secularism in its original sense is irrelevant for India. Another sense in which secularism has been used is the left definition: of the state as anti-religious. Some years ago, Marxist MPs objected to the Prime Minister inaugurating a public sector project by lighting lamps (that are in wide use in Hindu temples) and by breaking a coconut. They protested that these are Hindu symbols and a Prime Minister of a secular state should not indulge in them. This concept of secularism too we must reject. I may label it as the *Aggressive Left Secularism*. This variety of secularism has also been fostered in the country since 1969 by the partisan cultural patronage of Congress governments through communist leaning academicians, who are organized in Left-dominated institutions such as the Jawaharlal Nehru University and certain government funded research organizations. The aggressive Left secularism has many adherents amongst Muslim intellectuals too. It is a national tragedy for us all that after nearly six decades of independence, and after conceding Pakistan, Muslim intellectuals in India should see the choice before them increasingly as between Islamic Fundamentalism and Aggressive Left Secularism! There is however a middle ground between the two which Muslim intellectuals can take, and which a renaissance must encompass and foster. More about that later.

Enlightened Secularism thus means: [a] State neutrality to all religions; [b] equality of all religions before law; [c] uniform laws for all religions groups to adhere to; [d] that the majority has a special responsibility to foster harmony with minorities (if necessary by contract as with the Parsi community), but necessarily founded on the concept of mutual obligation. Minorities must thus stand up for majority concerns as well. Secularism cannot be a one-way obligation; [e] acceptance of Sanskritization process for cultural integrity.

I must however, emphasize here that the State and religion are separate. Although religion is the private concern of individuals, nevertheless the State should not enact laws or pursue policies in order to please religious orthodoxy. Instead I favour that the State create an atmosphere in which the people's resilience and their power to adjust themselves to change, is strengthened. The State should enact laws which, without interfering with the essential fabric of culture and religion, integrate society and promote a national outlook.

Renaissance of one religion is bound to have its effects on other religious faiths in the country. The status of women, for example, is already an issue exercising Hindus and consequently, by example, Muslims as well. The Hindu woman's agitation to function in society unfettered by oppressive customs, archaic marriage and inheritance laws, and dowry has had its effect on Muslim society as well. The progressive attitude of one religion is bound to affect the other religion. The brotherhood practiced by Islam, for example, has made Hindus re-examine their attitudes towards the scheduled castes in the wake of religious conversion.

It may however be easier to create conditions for a renewed Hindu Renaissance, than for a Muslim Renaissance. This is because the spiritual power centre of Islam is outside India. There is no Islamic spiritual authority residing in India, with powers to re-interpret the religious edicts in keeping with requirements of a renaissance. Therefore the State should not take any step which would bring forth the charge of interference in Islamic religious practices, save those which foster the concept of "equality before the law". For example, we can never agree that a woman witness is not equal to a man witness (Orthodox Islamic law requires two women witnesses to counter a man's evidence!). However, it is hoped that the *Ulemas* will themselves think about the need for progressive change in Muslim society, and move with the times. The *mullahs* of Muslim religion cannot demand that, for example, the personal laws of marriage and inheritance must follow the Shariat, but not the punishment for the penal offence of robbery (for Muslims this involves cutting off the hand at the wrist). If the Shariat is not to be implemented as a whole in India, (for example the Penal code is not to be Shariat based), then where and what is it to be truncated of the Shariat in other legal civil and criminal codes?

Thus secularism as defined and propagated till today, has lost its relevance. The concept, as understood by the masses of India stands thoroughly discredited. Hence the question is whether we should redefine secularism to make it acceptable to the masses or capitulate to the rising fundamentalism in the country.

When Martin Luther had defined secularism in Europe, it simply meant that the power of the State would be exercised independently of the directions of the Church. Thus, a secular Government would act to safeguard the nation-State, even if such action was without Church sanction. Later, Marx calling religion the 'opium of the masses', defined secularism to completely eschew religion.

In India, Jawarharlal Nehru and his followers subscribed to the later Marxist redefinition of the concept. This orthodoxy induced a reaction in the Indian masses. Nehru failed to define what historical roots ought to be a part of the modern India, and what was to be rejected. In the name of 'scientific temper', he rejected most of our past as 'obscurantism'. His orthodox secularism sought to alienate the Indian from his hoary past. Since more than 80 per cent of Indians are pan-Hindu in beliefs, and Hindu religion from its inception has been without a 'Church', 'Pope' or 'Book' (in contra-distinction to Christianity), therefore neither Martin Luther nor Marx made any sense to the Indian masses. Since there was little political challenge to Nehru after the untimely death of Gandhiji and Patel, the Marxian secularism concept superficially prevailed till his demise in 1964. The masses therefore humoured Nehru without accepting his concept of secularism. A conceptual void however remained to be filled.

But the Congress Party continued thereafter to fail to provide a political concept of secularism by which an Indian citizen could comprehend how he should bond "secularly" with another citizen of a different religion or language, or region and feel equally Indian. The Hindu instinctively could not accept the idea that India was what the British had put together, and that the country was just an area incorporated by the imperialists. Such a ridiculous idea, fostered quixotically by Jawarharlal Nehru University historians, found just no takers amongst the Indian people. The void remained thus, but the yearning in the masses to be Indian grew over the years with the growth of mass media. This void had therefore to be filled and the yearning of national identity required to be articulated for the masses.

It is my view that the real reason why secularism, as propounded by Nehru has floundered, is that it became an obstacle to the process called Sanskritization (from the word 'Sanskriti' or culture). Secularism as defined by Nehru froze the social order by either non-chalance or negative rebuke. It lacked the positive content of providing a process for assimilation, which is Sanskritization.

The Hindutva propounded by the RSS being the process of Sanskritization, has therefore attracted more the lower and deprived castes. In UP, the Yadavas, Kurmis and Lodhs, were the most enthusiastic adherents of Hindutva since it enabled Sanskritization through political empowerment.

Hence, Yadava leaders like Mulayam Singh, Kurmi leaders like Nitish Kumar and Lodh leaders like Kalyan Singh and Uma Bharati are feeling the heat of Hindutva and the pressure to conform. The RSS may be Brahmin-dominated at the leadership level, but its front organizations like the Bajrang Dal are mostly the Hindu proletariats.

Hence Sanskritization should be promoted by a call declaring the caste system as anti-Hindu. There is sufficient theological basis for such a call as Dr. M.V. Nadkarni has written (referred to above). He has made out a convincing case that birth-based caste system is actually against the tenets of Hindu religion.

Only such an approach can insulate the Indian mind from communal pollution and halt fascism. Indian culture needs modernization, but not westernization. We have to set religion to curb religious fanaticism in India.

Aggressive Left Secularism cannot do that because it is consistent only with an authoritarian Marxist state in which religion would be considered a subversive force. The religious fundamentalists are at the other extreme. They want that freedom of other religions be curbed, but that they themselves be given full liberty to interpret religion as they see it. This is possible only in a theocratic state. In India, Hindu obscurantists, of which mercifully there are only a few, view the rigid caste system, untouchability, the low status of women as even defensible, but take any Muslim practice to be fit for condemnation. For such extremists, the universal brotherhood practiced in Islam, is not worthy of emulation; but in fact is viewed as further evidence of the desirability of the caste system.

The fundamentalists among Muslims in India however are the preachers of a double standard. They are believers in *Reactionary Secularism*. They justify the discriminatory treatment meted out to the Hindus in Islamic countries, but want in the name of secularism all kinds of safeguards and guarantees for Muslims in India. For example, in Saudi Arabia, if any migrant worker is caught praying to any idol, or even celebrating Diwali, he is promptly arrested and cruelly sentenced. This, Muslim fundamentalists in India justify on the grounds that Saudi Arabia is an Islamic State. But the smallest curb on them in India, even in the name of secularism (*e.g.* the Supreme Court judgement in the celebrated Shah Bano case) brings the most violent protest from the Fundamentalists. Such double standards practiced by Muslim fundamentalists have now discredited the concept of secularism itself in the eyes of the Hindus and thereby strengthened reactionary and communal forces. That is why, I would label this as *Reactionary Secularism*.

But the spirit of secularism is good, and is consistent with our ethos. India's experience with theocracy in history was only during the Buddhist and Mughal periods. Generally, Hindu kings practiced the principle of secularism, different from the Aggressive Left and Reactionary varieties.

However, at the present juncture of our history, secularism conceptually needs to be redefined in the light of the experience of the last nearly six decades of Independence. Secularism cannot be used as a device to dissociate ourselves from the past, both good and bad. We must learn to cherish that which is glorious, and learn from that which was shameful. Such a secularism is based on a commitment to the brotherhood of religious communities, on their respect for and pursuit of truth.

Even on the question of the Shariat, the Muslim militants want the Indian State only to implement what suits them. They reject, the Shariat-ordained notion that a Muslim can have his hand cut off for the crime of robbery committed in India. How can a secular state accept such partial application? If Muslim fanatics in India can call for truncated application of the Shariat, where should such truncation stop. Why not include personal laws in such truncation?

UNIFORM CIVIL CODE FOR INDIA

The question whether India should adopt a uniform civil code should be treated as a legal question because it is a mandate addressed to the 'State' by Art. 44 under the Directive Principles of the Constitution.

Unfortunately, in India, legal questions are politicized when it affects the "Muslim vote bank".

Article 44 of the Constitution says –

> *"The State shall endeavour to secure for the citizens a uniform civil code throughout the territory of India."*

A controversy has however arisen as to the formation of a uniform code relating to the family or personal law of the parties relating to matters such as marriage and divorce, succession, adoption.

The framers of the Constitution clearly indicated what they meant by the word 'personal law' in Entry 5 of List III of the 7th Schedule of the same Constitution.

Entry 5 says:

> *"5, Marriage and divorce; infants and minors; adoption; wills; intestacy and succession; joint family and partition; all matters in respect of which*

parties in judicial proceedings were immediately before the commencement of this Constitution subject to their personal law."

The fathers of the Constitution had witnessed the baneful effects of a claim for separate identity of the Muslim community on the ground that their religion prescribed a separate personal law, — resulting in the lamentable Partition of India on the footing of the theory of 'Two Nations', founded on two religions. Hence, in the Constituent Assembly it was made clear that in a secular state personal laws relating to such matters as marriage, succession and inheritance could not depend upon religion, but must rest on the law of the land. A Uniform Civil Code was accordingly necessary for achieving the unity and solidarity of the nation [K.M. Munshi, VII C.A.D., 547-48]. Every time subsequently the question of Uniform Civil Code was raised by anyone in Parliament, the Government of India opposed it on the ground that to achieve it would be to hurt Muslim 'sentiments' and that no implementation of this Directive of the fundamental law could be made so long as the Muslims themselves would not come forward to ask for it. [see the statement made by former Prime Minister Mr. Rao in his Independence Day Speech at Red Fort on 15-8-1995. Nevertheless, the Supreme Court has recommended, more than once, that early steps must be taken towards the formulation of a Uniform Civil Code [Mudgal v. Union of India (1995) 3 S.C.C. 635 — Kuldip Singh & Sahai JJ].

That the Shariat is not infallible or immutable is evidenced by the patent fact that it has been discarded or modified in many respects by various Muslim States. And this has been achieved in an orthodox Muslim State such as Tunisia, through the process of liberal or progressive interpretation of the scriptures.

Advocates of immutability should be silenced by the following observations of a Muslim Judge of Pakistan, Huq, J., of the Lahore High Court—

"it would not be correct to lay it down as a positive rule of law that the present day Courts in this country should have no power or authority to

interpret the Quran in a way different from that adopted by the earlier Jurists and Imams. The adoption of such a view is likely to endanger the dynamic and universal character of the religion and laws of Quran."

The ground of immutability of the Shariat was in fact raised by some Muslim members in the Constituent Assembly of India but was rejected by Dr. Ambedkar. It would be an eye-opener to many today to recount what Ambedkar said [VII C.A.D. 5] in this context:

"... up to 1935 the North-West Frontier Province was not subject to Shariat law; it followed the Hindu law in the matter of succession and in other matters, so much so that it was in 1939 that the Central Legislature had to come into the field and to abrogate the application of the Hindu Law to Muslims of North-West Frontier Province and to apply Shariat Law to them ... apart from North-West Frontier Province, up till 1937 in the rest of India, in various parts, such as the United Provinces, the Central Provinces and Bombay, the Muslims to a large extent were governed by the Hindu Law in the matter of succession ... that in North-Malabar the Marumakkathayam law applied to all—not only to Hindus but also to Muslims." [op. Cit]

Even in India, the Koranic laws of crime and evidence have been supplanted as early as the 19th century by enacting the Penal Code and the Evidence Act, *e.g.*, by saving the Muslims from the following mediaeval atrocities which are still prevalent in Muslim countries like Pakistan and Bangladesh.

(*a*) Chopping off the hands of a criminal as a punishment for theft, or stoning to death as a punishment for adultery.

(*b*) Adultery and apostasy being punishable by death.

(*c*) Where the witnesses are women, their value as against the evidence of men is in the ratio of 2 : 1.

The entire law of criminal procedure has been replaced in India by statute.

The Indian laws of crimes and evidence make no distinction between Muslims and non-Muslims. The Judges in a Muslim dispute need not be Muslims.

In this context, one critic has pointed out that in Goa, from the days of Portuguese rule, the people have been governed by a uniform civil code, but Goanese Muslims have not lost their identity or culture. Hence now Parliament must legislate a Uniform Civil Code.

The Parliament of India has already superseded the Hindu law of marriage and succession, in the teeth of opposition from an enlightened section of Hindus. It was opposed by Dr. Rajendra Prasad himself on the grounds that Art. 44, being applicable to all persons in the territory of India, should not be imposed on the Hindus alone and that the Government who sponsored the Hindu Code Bill to replace the personal law of the Hindus had no mandate from the electorate in this behalf.

Above all, the Muslims who remained in India after the Partition did so with the full knowledge that divided India was going to adopt a Parliamentary system of democracy and not any Muslim system of the Middle Ages where Shariat would be the Supreme law of the land. They should also have known that a personal law founded on the religion of different communities was incompatible with the very concept of a 'Secular' State on which the new India was based.

Factually also, the assumption of the Government of India that the entire Muslim community is opposed to the implementation of Art 44 is not correct. The Shah Bano case demonstrated that it was only a section of the Sunni sect amongst the Muslims which was vehemently opposed to the judgement.

The Supreme Court can no more wash its hands off Art. 44 on the ground that it is a Directive Principle which is not directly enforceable. [Jorden v. Chopra (1985) 3 S.C.C. 62]. Besides, some Supreme Court Judges had expressed their views to the same effect out of Court: Gajendragadkar, C.J., and Chairman, Law Commission, in his book – *Secularism and the Constitution of India (1971)*, p. 126; Shelat, J., *Secularism, Principles & Application (1972)*; Hedge, J., in the Law Institute, in January, 1972;

Tulzapurkar, J., – article in A.I.R. 1987 Jours, 17; Beg. C.J., in his Motilal Nehru Lecture on 'Impact of Secularism on Life and Law'. In numerous cases, even prior to Kuldip Singh, J., the Supreme Court has remedied the inaction of the Government re other clauses of the Directive Principles to implement various Directives, in Articles 38, 39, 39A, 41, 42 and 43 of the Constitution of India by issuing 'directions' which are mentioned in Art. 32(2) as legitimate instruments in the hands of the Court.

Even in the matter of Art. 44, previous Benches of the Supreme Court had commented upon the inaction of the Government and the need for an early implementation of the Article –

(*a*) A unanimous Constitution Bench in the Shah Bano case (para. 32).

(*b*) A Division Bench, speaking through Chinnappa Reddy, J., in Jorden's case (cited above).

That the Shariat on personal law is not sacrosanct will appear from the following examples of Muslim majority countries which have superseded or modified polygamy.

Turkey: The Court can declare a second marriage as invalid on the ground that a spouse is living at the time of the second marriage [Turkish Civil Code, Art. 74].

Pakistan: A person cannot contract a second marriage without the permission of the Arbitration Council; and a wife can obtain divorce on the ground that the husband has married another wife.

Iran: A person cannot remarry without permission of the Court.

Egypt, Jorden, Morocco, Syria: Similar restrictions on bigamy as in Iran and Pakistan have been imposed in Egypt, Jordan, Morocco and Syria.

Tunisia: Bigamy is totally prohibited by the Tunisia Law of personal Status (s. 18).

Registration of all marriages, including those contracted in conformity with Shariat formalities, has been made compulsory in Iran, Algeria, Indonesia, Malaysia.

There is no reason why such law cannot be adopted in India.

The first feeling that we must inculcate therefore in our country is that all of us have an intimate connection with India's Hindu past. Eighty two plus per cent of India's population are, of course, Hindus, but even our largest minority, the Muslims should consciously accept that their ancestry is mostly Hindu. They have every right to remain good and true Muslims but they must learn not to condemn their Hindu past. This includes literature, sculpture, music, language, and the cultural aspects of our ethos. If today a Muslim for example learns Sanskrit, the Muslim Fundamentalists view him with suspicion, and regard him already half-way to becoming a Hindu. If a Muslim father names his son "Suryaprakash" instead of "Aftab", he would stand condemned in the eyes of these fundamentalists even though the two words mean the same.

In other words, reactionary secularism has been used as a cover for the Muslim Fundamentalists, to snap the organic ties of present day Muslims with their Hindu ancestry, thereby contributing to the further polarization of the two communities. Indonesia has shown that such a snapping of ties is not essential to Islamic beliefs.

India must remain committed to secularism, but this has to exclude the aggressive left as well as the reactionary versions. *Then what do we mean by secularism*? While Nehru, who popularized the word in India, meant it to be a commitment to anti-religiosity shaded with a "progressive" view of historical change, Gandhiji thought of it as the brotherhood of religious communities with a deep commitment to respect truth and to pursue it. The final test of Gandhi's secularism was truth, and the practice of secularism meant the pursuit of truth. *This is what I call enlightened secularism, and which we should accept as the definition of secularism in the Fundamentals for National renaissance.*

If Muslims truthfully accepted their Hindu ancestry, then certain problems that have recently caused great tension between Hindus and Muslims can be quickly resolved. It will also prevent the rise of the 'Politics of Cultural despair' which according to Prof. Fritz Stern led to Nazism in Germany. The *Ram Janmabhoomi* controversy would, for example, never have erupted. That for centuries, Hindus have patiently put up with what a lieutenant of Babar did to that holy spot does not mean that they do not have any depth of feelings about it (the evidence that Mir Baqi destroyed an existing temple to build the Babri Masjid is there with the Archaeological Survey of India since 1976 and reaffirmed in 2003 by a Commission set up on the direction of the Allahabad High Court). In fact, between 1193 A.D. (when Md. Ghori ransacked Ajmer) and 1729 A.D. when Quli Khan razed a temple to the ground in Tripura, about 80 major temples had been destroyed (as the maps below show), and thousands of smaller temples had been desecrated. In fact, there is a great stirring of Hindu consciousness today because of the utter disregard of Muslim fundamentalists for that feeling.

Instances of Temple Desecration

No.	*Date*	*Site*	*District*	*State*	*Agent*
	For nos. 1-24, see map 1: Imperialism of the Delhi Sultanate, 1192-1394				
1.	1193	Ajmer	Ajmer	Rajasthan	Md. Ghuri (s)
2.	1193	Samana	Patiala	Punjab	Albek (g)
3.	1193	Kuhram	Kamal	Haryana	Aibek (g)
4.	1193	Delhi		U.P.	Md. Ghuri (s)
5.	1194	Kol	Aligarh	U.P.	Ghurid army
6.	1194	Banaras	Banaras	U.P.	Ghurid army
7.	c. 1202	Nalanda	Patna	Bihar	Bakhtiyar Khalaji (c)
8.	c. 1202	Odantapuri	Patna	Bihar	Bakhtiyar Khalaji
9.	c. 1202	Vikramasila	Saharsa	Bihar	Bakhtiyar Khalaji
10.	1234	Bhilsa	Vidisha	M.P.	Iltutmish (s)
11.	1234	Ujjain	Ujjain	M.P.	Iltutmish
12.	1290	Jhain	Sawai Madh.	Rajasthan	Jalal al-Din Khalaji (s)
13.	1292	Bhilsa	Vidisha	M.P.	Ala al-Din Khalaji (g)
14.	1298-1310	Vijapur	Mehsana	Gujarat	Khalaji invaders
15.	1295	Devagiri	Aurangabad	Maharashtra	Ala al-Din Khalaji (g)
16.	1299	Somnath	Junagadh	Gujarat	Ulugh Khan (c)
17.	1301	Jhain	Sawai Madh.	Rajasthan	Ala al-Din Khalaji (s)
18.	1311	Chidambaram	South Arcot	Tamil Nadu	Malik Kafur (c)
19.	1311	Madurai	Madurai	Tamil Nadu	Malik Kafur

20.	c. 1323	Warangal	Warangal	A.P.	Ulugh Khan (p)
21.	c. 1323	Bodhan	Nizamabad	A.P.	Ulugh Khan
22.	c. 1323	Pillalamarri	Nalgonda	A.P.	Ulugh Khan
23.	1359	Puri	Puri	Orissa	Firuz Tughiuq (s)
24.	1392-93	Sainthali	Gurgaon	Haryana	Bahadur K. Nahar (c)

Source: Frontline [The Hindu], December 22, 2000

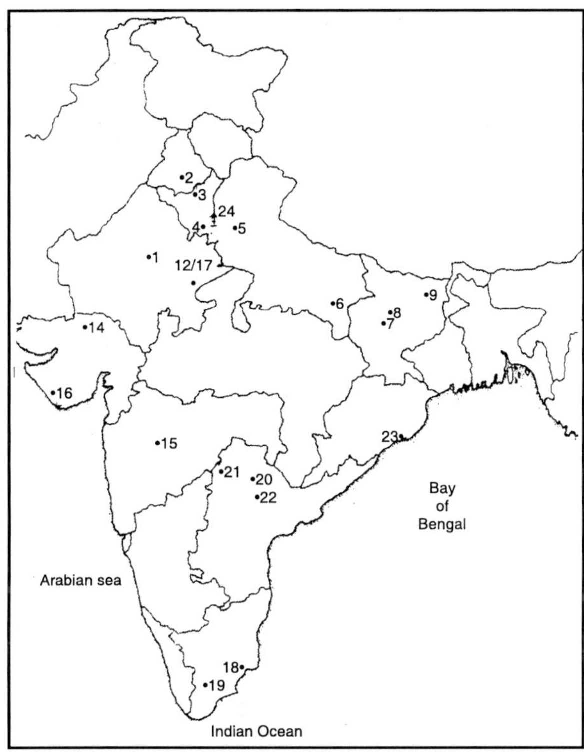

For nos. 25-55, see Map 2: Growth of regional Sultanates, 1394-1600

25.	1394	Idar	Sabar-K	Gujarat	Muzaffar Khan (g)
26.	1395	Somnath	Junagadh	Gujarat	Muzaffar Khan
27.	c. 1400	Paraspur	Srinagar	Kashmir	Sikandar (s)
28.	c. 1400	Bijbehara	Srinagar	Kashmir	Sikandar
29.	c. 1400	Tripuresvara	Srinagar	Kashmir	Sikandar
30.	c. 1400	Martand	Anantnag	Kashmir	Sikandar
31.	1400-01	Idar	Sabar-K.	Gujarat	Muzaffar Shah (s)
32.	1400-01	Diu	Amreli	Gujarat	Muzaffar Shah
33.	1406	Manvi	Raichur	Karnataka	Firuz Bahmani (s)
34.	1415	Sidhpur	Mehsana	Gujarat	Ahmad Shah (s)
35.	1433	Delwara	Sabar-K	Gujarat	Ahmad Shah
36.	1442	Kumbhalmir	Udaipur	Rajasthan	Amhmud Khalaji (s)

37.	1457	Mandalgarh	Bhilwara	Rajasthan	Mahmud Khalaji
38.	1462	Malan	Banaskantha	Gujarat	Ala al-Din Suhrab (c)
39.	1473	Dwarka	Jamnagar	Gujarat	Mahmud Begdha (s)
40.	1478	Kondapalle	Krishna	A.P.	Md. II Bahmani (s)
41.	c. 1478	Kanchi	Chingleput	Tamil Nadu	Md. II Bahmani
42.	1505	Amod	Broach	Gujarat	Khalil Shah (g)
43.	1489-1517	Nagarkot	Kangra	Him. P.	Khawwas Khan (g)
44.	1507	Utgir	Sawai Madh.	Rajasthan	Sikandar Lodi (s)
45.	1507	Narwar	Shivpuri	M.P.	Sikandar Lodi
46.	1518	Gwalior	Gwalior	M.P.	Ibrahim Lodi (s)
47.	1530-31	Devarkonda	Nalgonda	A.P.	Quli Qutb Shah (s)
48.	1552	Narwar	Shivpuri	M.P.	Dilwar Kh. (g)
49.	1556	Puri	Puri	Orissa	Suliman Karrani (s)
50.	1575-76	Bankapur	Dharwar	Karnataka	Ali Adil Shah (s)
51.	1579	Ahobilam	Kurnool	A.P.	Murahari Rao (c)
52.	1586	Ghoda	Poona	Maharashtra	Mir Mohd. Zaman (?)
53.	1593	Cuddapah	Cuddapah	A.P.	Murtaza Khan (c)
54.	1593	Kalihasti	Chittor	A.P.	I'tiber Khan (c)
55.	1599	Srikurman	Visakhapatnam	A.P.	Quth Shahi general

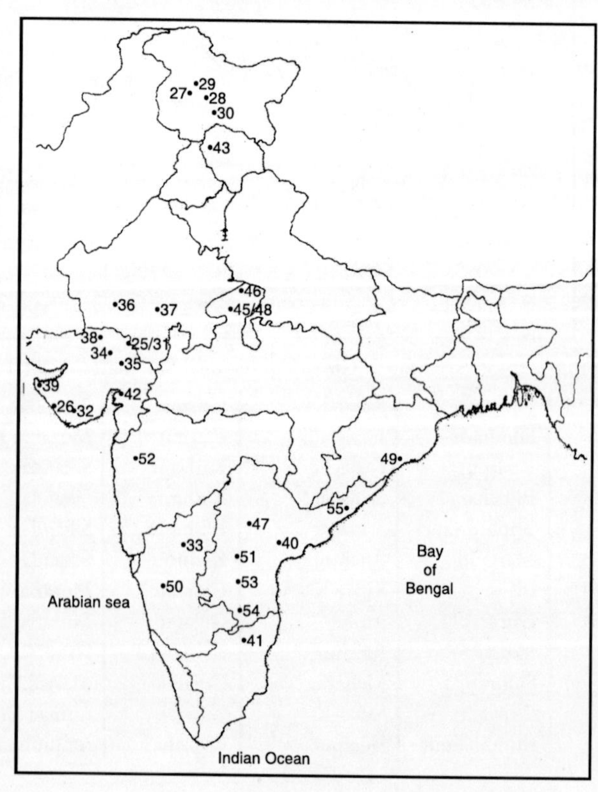

For nos. 56-80, see Map. 3: Expansion and Reassertions of Mughal Authority, 1600-1760

56.	1613	Pushkar	Ajmer	Rajasthan	Jahangir (e)
57.	1632	Banaras	Banaras	U.P.	Shah Jahan (e)
58.	1635	Orchha	Tikamgarh	M.P.	Shah Jahan
59.	1641	Srikakulam	Srikakulam	A.P.	Sher Md. Kh. (c)
60.	1642	Udayagiri	Nellore	A.P.	Ghazi Ali (c)
61.	1653	Poonamallee	Chingleput	Tamil Nadu	Rustam b. Zulfiqar (c)
62.	1655	Bodhan	Nizamabad	A.P.	Aurangzeb (p, g)
63.	1659	Tuljapur	Osmanabad	Maharashtra	Afzal Khan (g)
64.	1661	Cooch Bihar	Cooch Bihar	West Bengal	Mir Jumla (g)
65.	1662	Devalgaon	Sibsagar	Assam	Mir Jumla
66.	1662	Garhgaon	Sibsagar	Assam	Mir Jumla
67.	1664	Gwalior	Gwalior	M.P.	Mu'tamad Khan (g)
68.	1667	Akot	Akola	Maharashtra	Md. Ashraf (c)
69.	1669	Banaras	Banaras	U.P.	Aurangzeb (e)
70.	1670	Mathura	Mathura	U.P.	Aurangzeb
71.	1679	Khandela	Sikar	Rajasthan	Darab Khan (g)
72.	1679	Jodhpur	Jodhour	Rajasthan	Khan Jahan (c)
73.	1680	Udaipur	Udaipur	Rajasthan	Ruhullah Khan (c)
74.	1680	Chitor	Chityorgarh	Rajasthan	Ayrangzeb
75.	1692	Cuddapah	Cuddapah	A.P.	Aurangzeb
76.	1697-98	Sambhar	Jaipur	Rajasthan	Shah Sabz Ali (?)
77.	1698	Bijapur	Bijapur	Karnataka	Hamid al-Din Khan (c)
78.	1718	Surat	Surat	Gujarat	Haidar Quli Khan (g)
79.	1729	Cumbum	Ongole	A.P.	Muhammad Salih (g)
80.	1729	Udaipur	West	Tripura	Murshid Quli Khan

(e) = emperor (s) = Sultan (g) = governor (c) = crown prince

4.
The Third Fundamental:
The Strategy for Economic Reform in a Globalised World

By all accounts of visiting dignitaries and travelers spread over several centuries, India was, by the prevailing standards of those times a prosperous, developed country—and that as recently as 1780 AD. Perhaps the level of inequality and the extent of poverty of a section of the people was excessive, but nevertheless it remains a fact that the trade of the world with India flourished over several centuries because India was producing and trading what a large part of the world did not or could not produce. As a consequence, India enjoyed a "massive" balance of trade surplus with Europe, and with most other parts of the world. Merchants came from all over the world to purchase goods from Indian markets.

But by 1870, the economy entered into a long phase of decline, which decline by 1947 (*i.e.*, seven decades later), had transformed India from a pre-modern prosperous country to a poor under-developed nation judged by the modern industrial standards of the twentieth century. This unprecedented retrogression took place primarily because of the failure of Indian leadership to unite and harness scientific inventions, (such as the steam engine and blast furnace), for economic development—which the West had successfully done for itself. But the failure of Indian leadership was brought into abject reality by the heavy hand of British imperialism.

Tragically, India squandered a superb opportunity to develop quickly from 1947 onwards: during the Freedom Struggle, Mahatma Gandhi had built up leadership of quality at all levels, and there was a modicum of infrastructure, light industry and foreign reserves.

But alas, the adoption of the Soviet Model of centralized economic planning wasted all those advantages. The model was the anti-thesis of the Hindu concept of decentralization.

India's economic strategy was borrowed from the USSR and foisted on the Indian people in the Fifties by Jawaharlal Nehru – without much debate. *This was not the strategy that Mahatma Gandhi or Sardar Patel had advocated during the freedom struggle.* The author of this strategy, namely Nehru, wanted the Soviet model adopted for reasons not known to many, and paradoxically it suited the interests of two powerful vested groups within our country: one, the feudal compradors whose progeny during British rule received English education and then entered the bureaucracy through Civil Service examinations. The other group was Left-inspired Indian intellectuals educated in the thirties and forties in Oxford and Cambridge (the "Kim Philby" group). The latter group gave Nehru the necessary intellectual baggage, and used their friendship with Nehru, to secure posts in key points in government, press, academic and diplomatic service after India achieved independence in 1947.

The Soviet model was easily accepted in India largely because the 19th Century feudal class had graduated to the elite bureaucracy, and with the populist ideological cover provided by the Left entrenched at key points in the bureaucracy, politics, press, and academia, this feudal class found that under this model it continued to enjoy continued patronage power in the Indian economy. It was this firm grip on decision-making centres of the state apparatus that subsequently after independence, made the ideology of Mahatma Gandhi and Sardar Patel irrelevant at the political level, and relegated a personality like C. Rajagopalachari to the status of an American-inspired crank. There was little challenge elsewhere. Amongst political leaders, only Charan Singh had dared to question the appropriateness of the Soviet model. But he too could not make much headway because of the intellectual hostility of the Left-feudal combine. In fact, despite Charan Singh being one of the most well-read political stalwarts and a prolific writer on economics, he was dismissed in the media as a semi-literate kulak whose ideas were a mere re-hash of Adam Smith.

The grafting of this model on Indian planning was done by a physicist turned-statistician, who had little or no formal education in economics: Professor P.C. Mahalanobis, founder of the Indian Statistical Institute, Calcutta. Mahalanobis, a confirmed Left intellectual, had been inspired by a Soviet growth model of the 1920s authored by Fel'dman, and he introduced it into Indian planning.

The model was wholly unsuited to Indian economic conditions, because it was predicated on three untenable assumptions; that consumption could be postponed for an extended period and even curtailed; that agriculture would be in a position to provide funds for industrial growth; and that supply of capital goods would generate its own demand for it. The reality was opposite. In 1947, India had just emerged out of a terrible famine, a long Freedom Struggle, and a bloody Partition, not to mention a World War. The large masses of the rural people were either on the poverty line or below it. There was very little scope to tighten their belts. On the contrary, a steady increase in wage goods was necessary to raise standards of living. Agriculture during British imperialist rule had been bled to subsistence levels by the constant appropriations exacted by the British Indian colonial-landlord set-up. Agriculture was thus in no position to finance industrialization. In fact, the sector itself was in dire need of resources, if it was not to slide down further.

Be that as it may, it was the confluence of Nehruvian intellectual commitment to command economy and landed vested interests fostered by the comfortable feeling of the interest groups that planning would merely transfer power to marshall and dispose of resources from the right hand to the "left" hand. That is why the Left-leaning siblings of zamindars and the comprador class found no intellectual difficulty in adjusting to the "socialist pattern" of Indian society. Their foreign education positioned them in key places in the policy making apparatus of the Government to ensure that.

It is important to recognize that a comparison of countries with a common history reveals that those countries which adopted the Soviet economic model performed much more poorly than their counterparts who had adopted the market economic strategy. Table 4 below brings out this by comparing East with West Germany, and North with South Korea. In India too, as the data reveal (Table 3), while India achieved a higher GDP growth under the Soviet economic strategy than that under British imperialist rule, it nevertheless remained at an unimpressive average growth rate of 3.5 per cent. Thereafter, with progressive liberalization and economic reform, the growth rate accelerated.

Table 3: Growth Performance in the Five Year Plans

(*per cent per annum*)

		Target	*Actual*
1. First Plan (1951-56)		2.1	3.61
2. Second Plan (1956-61)	Soviet Model Period	4.5	4.27
3. Third Plan (1961-66)		5.6	2.84
4. Fourth Plan 91969-74)		5.7	3.30
5. Fifth Plan (1974-79)		4.4	4.80
6. Sixth Plan (1980-85)	Liberalization Period	5.2	5.66
7. Seventh Plan (1985-90)		5.0	6.01
8. Eighth Plan (1992-97)	Economic Reform Period	5.6	6.78
9. Ninth Plan (1997-2002)		8.0	6.20

Source: Planning Commission, New Delhi, April 2002.

Table 4: Economic Indicators—South/North Korea (1995-96) and West/East Germany (1989) Compared

	South Korea	North Korea	South/North ratio	West Germany	East Germany	West/East ratio
1	2	3	4	5	6	7
Population						
Million	44.9	23.9	1.9	62.1	16.6	3.8
GNP						
Billion $	451.7	22.3	20.3	1,207	96	12.6
Per capita income						
$	10,067	957	10.5	19,283	5,840	3.3
Economic growth						
In % p.a. 1990-1995	+7.6	-4.5	–	3.0	-0.8	–
Government expenditure						
Billion $	97.1	19	5.1	547.7	61.8	8.9
(as % of GNP)	(21.5)	85		(45.5)	(64.4)	
Defence expenditure						
Billion $	14.4	5.2	2.8	28.5	1.2	2.6
(as % GDP)	(3.2)	(23)		(2.5)	(1.6)	
per capita ($)	318	218	1.5	459	675	0.7
Foreign trade						
Billion $	260.2	2.05	126.9	61.1	47.0	13.0
(as % of GNP)	(57.6)	(9.2)		(50.6)	(49)	
Export of goods billion $	125.1	0.74	169	341.3	23.7	14.4
Import of goods billion $	135.1	1.31	103	269.8	23.3	11.5
Foreign debt						
Billion $	79	11.8	6.6	106.7	22	4.9
(as % of GNP)	(17.5)	(53)		(8.8)	(23)	
Life expectancy						
In years (1995)	72.0	70.5	1.02	75.0	74.0	1.01
Infant mortality						
Per 1,000 births (1995)	10	26	0.28	7.4	7.5	0.99
Rural population						
% of total (1995)	19	39	0.49	3.7	10.8	0.34
Radios[1]						
Per 1,000						
Inhabitants (1989)	1,003	207	4.9	83%	99%	0.84
Televisions[2]						
Per 1,000						
Inhabitants (1989)	207	14	14.8	94%	57%	1.65

Source: National Unification Board, Bank of Korea; Satistisches Bundesamt, Statistisches, Jahrnuchder DDR; Weltbank.

1. For West and East Germany: percentage of households with ratio.
2. For East and East Germany: percentage of households with colour television.

Thus, worldwide cross section data make for the clear inference that for fast economic development, the essential pre-conditions are democracy and market economy. To hide this fact, Leftist economists describe India's miserable growth rate of GDP at three and half percent per year, achieved under the pre 1991 Soviet model's Five Year Plans, as a "Hindu growth rate" that is a nation of Hindus cannot achieve a higher growth rate than that, no matter how wonderful was the Soviet System. Narasimha Rao as Prime Minister, however, demolished that myth by boldly liberalizing the economy and thus doubling the growth rate.

However, the Rao introduced reforms were *ad hoc* and not fundamental. They were a beneficial de-regulation in that it had helped free the Indian economy from suffocation of controls and licences. To make the economy healthy however, the nation needs today restructuring and reconstruction. We have not only to move more completely to a market economy, but we need new forms of governance of the market forces in a globalised framework that are consistent with the ethos of this ancient country. That means in tune with the enlightened Hindu cultural traditions. Otherwise, devoid of our moorings, we shall be manipulated by international forces. East Asian economies, for example, were booming in the 1980s and 1990s, but they had poor governance norms. One day in mid 1997, the US by manipulating the Wall Street bond market interest rates, set into motion a currency run and then a banking collapse. A major crisis resulted, from which East Asia has still to recover.

Hence, while we cannot opt out of the ongoing globalization process, still we have to ensure that within that process our economy is sufficiently insulated from international raiders and speculators. The globalization that we accept must also remain morally adequate. Globalization can alter values, spread disease more easily, and disrupt the family system that has been a great shock absorber in India against stress and uncertainty.

I must acknowledge that Pandit Deendayal Upadhaya had forseen the dangers of globalization and mechanical imitation of the West, long before even the process had started. In this "Integral Humanism" [1965], he outlined in embryonic form the new economic strategy that is consistent with the nation's *chitti*. Dattopant Thengadi, one of the most original thinkers of the post 1947 decades, following Deendayalji's ideas, had written a monograph on the conflict resolution required between market economy and Hindu human values. Based on his work, for the Friends of India Society International's 1978 New York conference I had re-stated Deendayalji's ideas in modern economic jargon in an article published by the conference organizers.

But thereafter, unfortunately, Gandhian Socialism took hold of the centre stage, and thus Integral Humanism could not be further developed into a comprehensive plan of action for national renaissance. Thus Nehruism had survived change of governments.

The time is now at hand to bury the remnants of the Soviet economic model for the future glory of India. We need to do that by adopting an alternative policy framework, for which Integral Humanism can be a beacon light.

Briefly stated, Integral Humanism recognized that in a democratic market economy, an individual has a technical freedom of choice; but the system, without safeguards, fails to accommodate the varying capabilities and endowments of the human being. Since the concept of the survival of the fittest prevails in such a system, therefore some individuals achieve great personal advancement while others get trampled or disabled in the ensuing "rat race". We need thus to build a safety net into our policy for the underprivileged or for the disabled while rewarding the meritorious and the gifted. Otherwise, the politically empowered poor in a democracy who are the majority will clash with the economically empowered rich who are the minority, thereby causing instability and upheaval in a market system.

Since maximum profit is enthroned as the goal in a capitalist system, the human being has to adjust to the terrific demands of technology rather than technology adjusting to the integral needs of mankind. Thus, a new economic strategy for national renaissance based on Integral Humanism, has to focus on enlightened governance and harmonious conflict resolution of the various human interests that drive the economy in different directions. Hindus have done it for centuries through varna ashrama dharma, in which the four sources of power: *Vidya, simhasan, dhana, and bhoomi* were not to be concentrated in any one person, but were dispersed. Unfortunately, the concept got corrupted by the adoption of birth-based caste system and untouchability, neither of which is in our vedic scriptures.

What does all this mean in practical terms? It means that in framing an economic policy consistent with our time tested value system, we must identify clearly our objectives, priorities, the strategy, the techniques of resources mobilization, and the institutional framework.

Table 5 : Alternative Economic Perspectives

Parameter	*Capitalism*	*Socialism*	*Communism*	*National Renaissance*
1. Objectives	Maximum profit welfare	Maximum material	Maximum production development	Optimum national
2. Priorities	Exploitation of resources	Guaranteed living standards	Primary of the system based on coercion	Primary of man through balanced development of 'purusharthas'
3. Development Strategy	Primacy of technology	Nationalization of commanding heights and public distribution	Total ownership of the means of production	Conflict resolution and harmony through complementaries
4. Resource	Incentive and propensity to spend	Taxation	Total control over incomes	Trusteeship and austerity
5. Institutional	Survival of the fittest laissez faire	Administrative controls, licences, and regulation	Dialectical Dialectical class struggle & annihilation	Dialectical Panchayat Raj, Self reliance, and market economy

The economic perspective for National Renaissance that we advocate is fundamentally different from the other competing ideologies: Capitalism, Socialism and Communism as Table 5 above summarizes. Capitalism and Communism have similarities in matters of objectives and institutional framework. If cost of production is stabilized, then maximum profit and maximum production are identical. Again, class struggle and annihilation, and survival of the fittest, are different only to the extent that Communism envisages the survival of the 'fittest' class, whereas Capitalism expects the 'fittest' individual to engage in fierce competition and annihilate the other rivals. Similarly, Socialism has only a *difference of degree* with Communism – on the extent of coercion and control, and not in any fundamental respect. That is why Communism is referred to by Karl Marx as "scientific" Socialism, although there is nothing scientific about it. Since one Socialism differs from another Socialism only in degree, therefore there are unlimited varieties of Socialism varying from those of Hitler's Nazism, to Jawaharlal Nehru's Socialism, to the democratic Socialism of Sweden. This has only caused confusion and given ample scope for hyprocrisy!

I need not dwell any further on the demerits of other ideologies, but consider in concrete positive terms, what steps should be taken for the rapid economic growth and development of the nation.

India becoming a developed country and world power by 2020 is feasible if we ensure that:

[a] the GDP grows at an average of 10% per year for the ten years from 2008 onwards, and 7% thereafter till 2020. This growth has to be achieved within the framework of globalization, which process has become inevitable, irresistible, and irreversible. But globalization has opportunities and risks. India has therefore, to make participation in globalizaion, socially tolerable and morally adequate.

[b] education is fostered to empower the people with IT savy self-employment skills, and also to develop a secular patriotic ethos that courageously resists fundamentalism and terrorism. Such an orientation will enable the country to remain focused on development issues.

[c] harmonious international alliances are effected on various levels of bonding—such as cultural (with SAARC, Afghanistan, Burma and ASEAN), strategic (such as with China, Isreal, and Iran), contractual (such as with the United States *e.g.*, help US in Iraq), and develop pre-emptive contingency plans (*e.g.*, if the Pakistan President is dislodged by Taliban).

The first requirement can be met if we are able to raise the rate of investment from the current 24 per cent of GDP to 30 per cent while increasing the efficiency in the use of capital by reducing the capital output ratio from the present 4.0 to 3.0. How this level of investment can be achieved is a policy challenge. Increased investment can be effected for example, by abolishing income tax and by simplifying excise and custom duty levies. This will raise the rate of domestic saving but it will require a major overhaul of the Budgeting process. We can add to this level of investment by more FDI for which it will require that we deregulate more and create world-class infrastructures, even if in pockets such as in SEZs. Although India may have low labour costs, this is offset by high transaction costs caused by delays, a socialistic labour law and corruption. Streamlining procedures through e-governance will help cut transaction costs, but this too will require a major attitudinal change in bureaucracy. All this will imply the need for second generational reforms.

This is however the supply side of the equation. On the demand side to match the rise of goods and services implicit in the 10 per cent growth rate of GDP we need to aggressively export. This can be done by exploiting our comparative advantage which requires developing a new work culture of honouring contracts, work culture of keeping to schedules, and transparency in decision making. We should have to foster the ethos of risk taking, shaking off the socialist hangover of personally seeking a secure future at all costs. At present, Indians prefer guaranteed poverty to a risky prosperity. We should also adopt policies such as inter-linking of rivers and other mega projects to put purchasing power at the earliest with the common people so that not only assets are created, and there is greater economic integration, but the poor come to feel that they too have a place in the Vision 2020.

With the developing new concepts in business of co-creation between firms and consumers [as expounded by Prahalad and Ramaswamy in *Future of Competition* (Double Day, 2004)], globalization has become crucial for India's development.

Globalization may be defined as the process of re-location, restructuring and outsourcing of productive economic activity characterized by more and more free movement of factors of production, knowledge, technology and services, and by the mutual interaction and effects of such movements. It marks a decisive shift in the proportion of the world output being produced in a trans-national framework.

Today, globalization is a powerful and fast emerging global reality that has already acquired an irresistible momentum of its own. At present about one-fifth of the gods produced in the world are traded internationally, and about US $ 1.5 trillion is exchanged daily in currency markets. It is a theme of this address that each country should devise its own strategy that takes into account local factors and constraints to "sail with the wind" of globalization, in the direction that this strategy sets, rather than confront the process itself and tilt against the wind. There are in such an approach advantages that have to be seized and maximized as well as risks that have to be addressed and minimized.

It is to be noted that while growth in GDP and trade vastly accelerated with each stage of globalization, world income however has become much more unequally distributed. The ratio of the income accounted by the top 20 per cent of nations of the world to that for the bottom 20 per cent, rose from 3 : 1 in 1820 to 30 : 1 in 1970 to 86 : 1 in 1998. This trend can continue into the 21st century, since the globalization process, as structured today, will create fault lines between groups of nations that have, and those that have not, the skills and mobility to flourish in the knowledge based information technology paradigm. Unless these fault lines are repaired, the widening disparity amongst nations will continue at an even faster pace because of which the world will risk social unheaval. And since these fault lines are replicated within nations, between educated elite and non-elite groups, the same potential for upheaval will exist internally too. Thus more than the spread and accessibility to capital, what is required in the new stage of globalization is the dissemination of knowledge and know-how to the poor and under privileged. How this will be done is an essential part of coping with globalization's negative impact.

The question here is how to meet the challenge of these trends in globalization and how countries like India can figure and fit in it. There is no doubt that developed countries are today led by the United States and collectively dominate this globalization process. Furthermore, nowadays a large number of developing countries follow the lead of the US. This can be seen today in any international conference. Hence, there is a challenge for countries like India and China, ancient nations that cannot be followers, but which are not yet sufficiently economically developed to be by themselves significant factors to command either co-option by the developed countries, or in the alternative be in a position to form a parallel economic order.

One thing is perfectly clear to me, that is, it is not wise to opt out of the globalization process today since the process has already acquired a near universal acceptance and almost an irresistible momentum. The WTO, for example, has a membership of 146 countries, as of 1.1.04, who are ready to accept its rigorous rules, and thus enjoy automatically, the mutual Most Favoured Nation (MFN) status. To exit the WTO would hence mean negotiating bilateral trade treaties for exports, a horrendous and tough exercise, in which there will be few takers ready to sign such treaties leave alone grant MFN status.

Hence, it is prudent to stay with the globalization process and search for ways and means to carve out one's own corner and niche in it. That is what I advocate for my country. (I dare say that the logic for India applies in large measure to Iran too for the same reason as I will summarise below). This is one parameter that has to be a marker or "bottom line" to meet the challenge of globalization. Not to quit!

Globalization has five dimensions: Internationalization of production, liberalization of regulations, universal standardization of weights, measures, and quality, de-territorialisation and westernization of tastes. In order to make the process socially tolerable and morally adequate in all the five dimensions, The Indian and Iranian civilizations have a special responsibility in spelling out the boundaries and its markers within which the process of globalization will be circumscribed. Unbridled globalization will most likely erode the binding sense of community, interpersonal trust, and the traditional family-based acceptance of responsibility of the underprivileged that is the hallmark of Indian and Iranian society. This is because the implied acquisitive and materialistic individualism which is at the core of unbridled globalization, undermines the values of social conscience or even tribal loyalties that exist in traditional cultures.

Hence, in the name of sailing along with the globalization process, it is imperative that *Laissez Faire* is not adopted. On the contrary, it is all the more essential that the State step in as and when it is necessary to prescribe limits to the reach of globalization and impose reasonable justiciable restrictions to correct the abuses. Survival of the fittest, the core of *Laissez Faire*, must decisively be rejected as a social doctrine. Modern society has to provide safety nets for the weak or under privileged.

This parameter in the strategy to meet the challenge of globalization will require a new governance that requires a very alert government because globalization means much greater financial volatility, shorter boom bust cycles, employment insecurity due to relocation, and even health hazards such as from AIDS: in 1996, there was just one case of HIV positive in India; in 2004, it was 5 million! All these leave a very short reaction time for Government intervention. The potential of destabilized economies due to globalization is thus large and hidden. The East Asia Crisis of 1997 and the recent Argentinean crisis are clear warning signals in this regard. Hence, in a globalized world, governments will have to have a major role of being effective shock absorbers, fire fighters and even to police occasionally, the course of development. The question, therefore, is not one of downsizing or upsizing the government anymore but one of "right sizing" to meet the challenge of globalization.

To come on par with the US by say 2050, India will have to deploy its young population to tap future innovations. As the President of India, Dr. Abdul Kalaam has observed, in the coming years, peoples lives will be enriched by IT-driven knowledge products and systems, biotechnology, and space technology. We may fund human-beings inhabiting a planet other than the earth and solar power being beamed down to earth. Moreover, hypersonic vehicles, with speeds of more than Mach 10, will fly across continents and will also be used for weapons delivery. Human life will be further prolonged through genomic and biotechnological research. An area holding even greater promise is that of edible vaccine. This would be a boon to India as millions of its people get affected by diseases like Polio and Hepatitis-B. A plant system for delivering the vaccine needs to be developed.

Nanotechnology will enter human usage in the shape of control mechanisms of various transporting systems, medical equipment, and aerospace systems like micro satellites, mini RPV. Another area of human concern in the coming decades would be the pattern of global energy dependence. Table 6 below indicates the technology for the next fifty years.

Table 6 : Connectivity in the future

1. Physical Connectivity	Roads, transport, airports, ports, quality power
2. E-Connectivity	Internet network, telecom, health, education, agriculture, e-commerce
3. Knowledge Connectivity	Classy infrastructured schools, professional institutions.
4. Market Connectivity	Access to globalized world and determination to participate
5. Welfare Connectivity	Health, Pension, Social Security, and Safety Nets
6. Government Connectivity	Transparency, governance, better and cleaner politics

Thus the main pre-requisite for India becoming a world power is to have a developed economy that is well integrated with global markets. Trade, FDI and financial leveraging are essential for rapid growth of the Indian economy, at 10 per cent per year in Gross Domestic Production or GDP at least for a decade. Defence expenditure should be pegged at 7% of GDP, with the dominant share for Navy, R&D and weapons acquisition.

That means that in the next three years the growth rate has to rise from the current 7% to 10%, and then be sustained at that level for the subsequent ten years.

Thereafter till 2020, the economy should be sustained at 7 per cent annual growth rate in GDP. Technically, this requires a rate of investment of 30 per cent of GDP (up from 24%) and an incremental capital-output ratio (ICOR) of 3.0 (down from 4.5). The rate of investment can be raised by either the domestic saving rate (presently 22%) or foreign investment (2% currently) or both. ICOR can be reduced only by decreasing the inefficiency in the current allocation of capital and by raising total productivity. These require new reforms to solve the problems of: (*i*) Financial Debt-Trap (*ii*) Budget Strait jacket (*iii*) Crowding out private investment by Government borrowing from banks (*iv*) De-regulation at State and local levels (*v*) Poor Infrastructure: power & roads (*vi*) High transaction costs of corruption and delays.

What kind of reforms are required? Reforms have not only to improve efficiency, but also must motivate the people and integrate local markets nationally and national market globally. Such reforms would generate employment for the masses, and hence create commitment of voters for more reforms.

The main reform areas are therefore as indicated in the following charts:

Three Key Barriers Constrain India's Growth—CAGR (2000-2010)

- Small scale reservations
- FDI restrictions
- Poor regulations
- High import duties
- Unequal taxes

- Central PSUs
- State PSUs including power
- Municipal services

10.1

0.3

0.7

1.3

2.3

5.5

- Unclear titles
- Tenancy laws
- Low property taxes and low user charges

India (status quo)

Product market barriers

Land market barriers

Government ownership

Others barriers:
- Labour market
- Roads & ports infrastructure

India (Complete reforms)

Source : McKinsey Consultants, New York, 2001.

The Government Needs to Focus On 13 Key Actions (1/2)

Category	*Decisions*	*Key sectors directly affected*
Product Market	1. Remove reservation of products for small-scale industry	• 836 manufactured goods
	2. Equalise sales tax and excise duty for all categories of companies within sectors and strengthen enforcement	• Manufacturing (*e.g.*, steel & textile) • Retail trade • Restaurants and hotels
	3. Develop effective regulatory framework and strong regulatory bodies	• Power • Telecom • Water supply
	4. Remove licensing and quasi-licensing restrictions that limit the number of players in an industry	• Dairy processing • Sugar mills • Petroleum marketing • Banking • PF management
	5. Reduce import duties to ASEAN levels (10 per cent) over 5 years	• Manufacturing (*e.g.*, automotive)
	6. Allow FDI in retail and remove limits on FDI in all sectors	• Retail • Telecom • Insurance

Source: McKinsey analysis

The Government Needs to Focus On 13 Key Actions (2/2)

Category	*Decisions*	*Key sectors directly affected*
Land market	7. Sort out unclear property titles	• construction
	8. Raise property taxes and user charges for municipal services and lower stamp duties	• Retail trade • Restaurants and hotels
	9. Reform tenancy laws to allow rents to rise to market levels	
Government ownership	10. Privatise SEBs, all PSUs and municipal services — Start with the largest companies — Target around 30 companies a year	• Power • Banking • Insurance • Manufacturing and mining • Airlines and road transport
Other	11. Reform labour laws by repealing section 5-B of the Industrial Disputes Act; Introducing standard retrenchment – compensation norms; allowing full flexibility in the use of contract labour	• Labour intensive manufacturing
	12. Contract out construction of roads to "lowest-subsidy" bidder. Contract out the management of existing roads, ports and airports (*e.g.*, Cochin airport)	• Roads • Ports • Airports
	13. Strengthen agricultural extension services for improving agricultural yields	• Agriculture

Source: McKinsey analysis

5.

The Fourth Fundamental:
National Security Doctrine for Global Reach

If a market-oriented economy that fosters self-reliance in individuals and protects the weak through a safety net is ideal for renaissance, *an effective national security doctrine in which the goal is to defend the assets of the nation and to achieve for India a polar position in the international power structure, is best suited for the country and conducive for our national renaissance.* The national security of a nation is however a composite of the GDP, defence capability, effective and innovative population, technological capacity, national health, and environmental stability.

India has the capacity to be a great power, with a large geographical continent size, location strategically placed, and a huge, talented population with the world's third largest scientific and engineering manpower. But does the Indian nation have the collective 'Will' to exercise power in order to realize India's potential to its fullest capacity? Unfortunately, this Will has been sorely lacking over the last six decades of Independence. This is because of our identity crisis.

For ending this crisis, Indians with one mind must acknowledge that our civilization rests on a Hindu foundation, and that India is a nation of Hindus, those whose ancestors were Hindus, and those other minorities who accept Hindu culture, such as the Parsis. Hence India may be called Hindustan.

Throughout history, the great kings in ancient Hindustan were conscious of the innate greatness of the land, and thus they exercised power commensurate with the size of the country. The Cholas in South India became great naval powers, and spread India's influence to Indonesia, Kampuchea and Vietnam. In more recent time, Shivaji controlled the Arabian Sea, while Maharaja Ranjit Singh extended Indian influence and control over Afghanistan. There was a distinctive character of this influence: India's established links that were also civilizational, religious and cultural.

At the commencement of the new millennium of the 10 largest economies in terms of size measured by GDP in PPP rates, the USA is the largest economy, the next largest economy China, the third largest economy Japan, with India as the fourth. The next five positions are taken by the big four of Europe: Germany, UK, France and Italy. Brazil and Russia bring up the rear with their joint size less than that of India.

Before the end of the current decade, India's economy will become larger than that of Japan, thus taking it to 3rd place behind the USA and China. China, India and the USA are already the three most populated countries of the globe.

The projected changes in the relative size of economies will have profound implications for global governance, the global balance of power and the stability of Asia as the Pakistani economist Shahid Burki has observed recently. The phenomenal change in the implied power structure will pose a major challenge to Europe, N. America, and even to Asia itself, that few seem to really comprehend or even appreciate today. There is confidence today that India can make it. Moreover, India after 2015 will be uniquely placed to harness 'a demographic dividend' with a population of median age of 29 years compared to China (37 years) and Japan (48 years).

There are several *alternative scenarios* on where India could be in the year 2020, which fall between two extremes. On one extreme is the optimistic scenario of India becoming a developed, united and secure nation, with adequate military power and a UN Security Council seat with a veto, a nation with no significant poverty, unemployment, environmental or health hazards. On the other extreme is a pessimistic scenario in which India collapses and balkanizes like the USSR, Yugoslavia, Lebanon, or fragments like Colombia into separate countries or areas with rampant terrorism, narcotic rackets & AIDS, stark poverty, and unemployment.

India has already been through the pessimistic scenario once in the eighteenth and nineteenth centuries. The case of Yugoslavia and the USSR in the 20th century shows that we can do so again in the 21st century. Hence there is a "choice" for Indians to make: which route to take? Merely wishing to be a developed country by 2020 is not enough. We have to work for it.

India could overtake China, and come abreast of the USA by 2050 provided this nation can overcome the imminent budgetary crisis. It is imminent because government's fresh borrowing capacity is soon going to shrink below, and fall short of, the repayment of past loans received and that the allocation of resources to immutable heads such as defence, subsidies, pensions and police becomes equal to government revenues, leaving no resources for any investment. The state governments are already bankrupt and depend on doles from a near insolvent Centre. To break out of this world requires a new dynamic modern political leadership that Indian democracy has proved capable of providing—but as in the past, *after* a crisis (*e.g.*, food (1967) and balance of payment crisis (1991)).

Is the optimistic scenario realistic or feasible for the India of today? Yes, if we adopt the correct ideology and policies today. The last six decades of Independence are replete with examples of how we have adopted wrong policies, which were out of sync with the

Nation's endowment, that we could rectify each time *only after a crisis*. The suppression of the agricultural sector for example in the five year plans was stopped only after the Food Crisis of 1966-67. The authoritarian trends in the state were laid to rest only after the Emergency Crisis in 1975-77. The disastrous Soviet model was dismantled only after the Balance of Payments (BoP) Crisis in 1990-91. Therefore, we should now learn from experience and not wait for another crisis for adopting the correct policies necessary to make India a developed country by 2025.

To begin with, the people will have to elect a meritorious and modern leadership who are modern, patriotic and rooted, in India's glorious past. For this, the electorate will have to rise above caste fanaticism and religious bigotry and to vote accordingly. Governments provide governance and leadership, and in the highly sophisticated world of today, India needs modern minded leaders.

If such a leadership indeed comes to office, what needs to be done? *First of all*, we need to consciously adopt a national security doctrine that defines our security goals, fixes priorities, determines defence strategy and integrates the requirements of defence, development and diplomacy into a coherent doctrine. Pending that blissful occurrence when all nuclear weapons can be destroyed, in order to enforce such a doctrine in practical terms, we shall have to acquire nuclear weapons with a delivery system. This must be backed by credible retaliatory strategy to constitute a deterrence. Our technological capacity for this acquisition is already there. This acquisition is an insurance against nations, big and small, far and near, who might threaten us with those kinds of weapons. Possession of nuclear weapons is also " an international driver's licence" to permit us to navigate in the world arena. Furthermore, if our doctrine is to be taken seriously. India should demonstrate that it can stand on its own feet and exercise power whenever its interests, near and far, are jeopardized. India should be ready to despatch military forces anywhere where anti-Indian ethnic clashes endanger human rights. This will be a demonstration of willingness to use power in all its dimensions to secure our national interests. And once such force is despatched, we should pay the price to ensure the peaceful existence of the overseas Indian Community. This we have repeatedly failed to do in the past *e.g.* when the IPKF retreated from Sri Lanka. In Sri Lanka, we should not hesitate to create Eelam—as we did with regard to Bangladesh—*if that is the only way* to safeguard the Tamils. But it must be clear, that for Eelam we cannot empower the terrorists. If Eelam is to be created at all, it has to be under Indian patronage. Similarly, we should defend Indians in Fiji, South Africa, Guyana and other places where they are targeted just because they are of Indian origin.

Thus drawing on the theory of games, a national security doctrine must define strategic issues, determine the relevant players in each issue, identify each player's strategic goals, determine the potential actions for each player, and decide the likely structure of the power game such as whether actions will be sequential, simultaneous, one-shot or escalated etc.

But we cannot play this 'game' unless we acquire an effective power that will make the other powers feel the consequences of that power. One way for example, to make such power felt, is to develop the Indian navy in a big way, to control the sea lanes between our Nicobar islands and Sumatra in Indonesia. Over 90 per cent of the economic world powers' commercial sea-traffic passes through the narrow (90 miles) Malacca Strait. If we can develop naval power to the point where we can police this strait, it will give India enormous power and leverage to influence international events. This has diplomatic implications. It is obvious, for example, that we cannot control the Malacca strait without the active cooperation of Indonesia. However through proper diplomatic moves we can obtain Indonesia's cooperation and forge a strategic relationship with that country because we have long historical links with these islands through our cultural links of the past.

India's national security goal thus is clearly to deploy power optimally for: (1) the maintenance of Hindustan's unity and integrity, *and recovery of lost territories*, (2) the preservation and sustenance of the core values of the nation state of Hindustan which are enshrined in our Constitution, such as democracy, an enlightened secular society, a federal polity, an egalitarian order, and moral Hindu cultural values, (3) safeguarding peace on our borders, (4) ensuring internal security for economic growth and (5) defending all people of Indian origin anywhere in the world, who are denied basic human rights.

To implement a national security doctrine with such objectives we shall have to take a holistic inter-disciplinary approach to devise a concrete national security strategy. This can be achieved by strengthening the national security council with civilian, military, and specialist personnel, *which interacts with inter-ministerial groups* to continuously formulate options for an apex political body like the Cabinet Committee on Political Affairs (CCPA) to take decisions on national security issues. At present we do not have such an effective organization, nor has any effort been made to date, to assess our national security needs in this comprehensive and integrated way.

National security is a function of a country's external environment and the internal situation, as well as their interplay with each other. The former is influenced by the major features of the prevailing international order, the disposition of its immediate and extended neighbours and the major powers. The internal situation encompasses many aspects of national life, ranging from law and order to economic fundamentals and from the quality of governance to national cohesiveness. The external environment and internal situation of a country do not subsist in watertight compartments but act and react on each other in ways which affect its security. In today's interdependent world, the distinction between internal and external security concerns often gets blurred.

The traditional concept of national security has undergone fundamental changes over the years. It is no longer synonymous with sufficient military strength to defend the nation and its interests. In today's world, military might alone does not guarantee either sovereignty or security. The more comprehensive approach to national security also includes economic strength, internal cohesion and technological prowess. The fundamental security of the individual citizen includes security of life and property, food security, energy security, clean environment, education and health. A clear sense of national identity and good governance also forms an integral part of national security; as does the ability to retain political and economic sovereignty and autonomy of decision making, in an era of globalization and increasing economic interdependence.

Both the external and internal environment are changing at an incredibly fast pace, with developments in nuclear weapons and missiles, increasing cross-border terrorism, the emergence of 'non-state actors', the growth of religious fundamentalism, the narcotics-arms nexus, illegal migration and left wing and ethnic extremism, impacting upon the security of the country. The rapid technological developments underway at the same time not only facilitate these events by reducing our reaction time but they also add entirely new dimensions of threats and challenges.

Amidst these dramatic developments, the traditional structures and processes for the management of national security are under considerable stress. Not only are most of them nearly 60 years old but their effectiveness has also, over time, been feeble. The national security establishment needs to be suitably restructured and strengthened, to cope with the new and emerging challenges facing us in the areas of Intelligence, Internal Security, Border and Defence Management, so as to help develop a more efficient and cost effective national security system for the 21st century to facilitate national renaissance.

India despite being a billion strong in population and a world leader in software and computer technology, has instead become over the years, a beleaguered nation state, haplessly trying to put out the fire of terrorism and secessionism in every corner of India. Today, about 40 per cent of the Indian army is deployed directly or indirectly in restoring civil order. New areas of possible insurgency are opening up suddenly. The LTTE backed Tamil extremists, for example, now flushed with ransom money obtained from bandit Veerappan, and with its stooges in ministerial office at the Centre, are positioned today to strike at the civil order in the state of Tamil Nadu; and with their compact with PWG, ULFA, Naxalites, Maoists and Pakistan's ISI, they can create a serious disorder.

While erosion of the might of the Indian state has taken place steadily over the last six decades, the last ten years have seen a significant acceleration in that depressing downward trend. The alarming undermining of the sovereignty of the state began in early 1990, with the capitulation of the V.P. Singh government in the Rubaiyya kidnapping case. Incidentally, all the main surviving personna are now in the National Front crowd.

The capitulation in the Rubaiyya kidnapping episode, in the releasing of five hard core extremist prisoners for her release, in one blow raised the image of the enemies of the state as heroes who could make the government of nearly 1 billion Indians bend before them. Not since the defining Battle of Plassey in 1757 did India seem so patently vunerable to an offensive by so few. That there was an alternative to this capitulation was demonstrated when the successor Chandrashekhar government (in which I was a Minister) perched precariously in a minority in Parliament, nevertheless refused to yield in a similar situation. On February 27, 1991 (a week before the Government collapsed) former Union Minister Saif-uddin Soz's daughter Nehma Intiyaz was similarly kidnapped by the JKLF and a similar ransom demanded. But her release was obtained within a week and without any quid pro quo, by tactics that have to remain secret for now. Her abductor was caught too, and convicted recently by a CBI Special Court. This proved that even a tottering government is only so weak as the mental softness its leadership and is not dependent, on its numeric stability. Regrettably, the Chandrashekhar government did not last long enough (it fell on March 11, 1991 and demitted office on June 21, 1991), to consolidate this message of innate toughness of the Indian State.

During the 1990s, the Indian state has also been under siege from the menace of the LTTE-ISI nexus. The LTTE-ISI nexus has ramification for Indian security, in four dimensions: *First*, their common hatred of India translates itself into undermining the Indian political system. Assassinations, bribery and honey trapping of key Indian personalities in politics, media, and academia are its tools in this subversion. In this way, the LTTE-ISI nexus has now acquired a wide network in India. By recruiting underworld dons, and recycling their ill gotten funds through key Indian corporate houses that are cash-strapped, another dimension of this stratagem of the nexus has been effective. *Second*, the LTTE-ISI nexus is interacting with and giving training to every secessionist, terrorist and sub-ethnic outfit in India. LTTE trains the ULFA, the PWG and the Naxalites in sabotage and weaponry. Balkanization of India is the nexus' goal. The episode of the Veerappan kidnapping of Raj Kumar, the cine actor, has confirmed my repeated warning on the nexus between the LTTE and Tamil separatists. *Third*, the LTTE-ISI nexus masterminds the cash rich narcotics trade from Afghanistan to Chennai enroute to Europe and USA, with a stop over in their strong holds of Palermo and Milan in Italy. Like AIDS, narcotics can sap and ruin the verve and energy of any flourishing nation, as testified by the pathetic state today of the erstwhile 'model Latin American nation' of Colombia. *Fourth*, the ISI-LTTE nexus has carried out terrorist acts to demonstrate the impotence of the Indian leadership whereafter through their network they have undermined the self-esteem of the Indian people. Nothing has eroded the esteem of India, as much as the ISI facilitated Indian Airlines Airbus hijacking, and the Indian government's capitulation in Kandhahar, when to rescue the hijacked Indian Airlines passengers, the External Affairs Minister Mr. Jaswant Singh personally escorted on a special air force plane, five deadly terrorists taken out from judicial custody in an Indian prison, (and that too, without a court order). Such a chaperoning of the enemies of the nation by the custodians of the Indian state is unprecedented. During my recent visit to Pakistan, one informed source told me that in addition $ 50 million was paid as ransom.

The question today, therefore, is whether there is a way to lift the siege the Indian state is under, and rescue the nation from the current trend towards being undermined completely.

The first and foremost resolve of patriotic Indians has to be that the Indian state will not negotiate with terrorists. By this standard, it was damaging to the national fabric to have negotiated with the hijackers in Kandhahar. Instead the government should have counter threatened the Taliban, and the hijackers with tactical nuclear weapons if any Indian passenger aboard the abducted aircraft was harmed. We should subsequently have pursued the hijackers with the same determination and stamina as the US government did with the Libyan subversives who masterminded the blowing up of the Panam Boeing 747 aircraft over Lockerbie in Scotland. In the same vein of national resolve, the union government should have despatched our elite Israeli-trained commandos to storm LTTE supremo V. Prabhakaran's Mullaitheevu hideout where he is coolly sitting at a stone's throw from Rameshwaram.

Second, the nation has to recognize that the root of terrorism in India and the undermining of the nation state, is the ISI-LTTE nexus. *Our short term goal ought to be to break this nexus.* India should attempt that by directly talking to Pakistan, mobilising the US, and most of all applying to China for help. Such talking should carry a sting [such as hot pursuit of terrorists, or pre-emptive bombing of camps], and a determination to administer it if necessary. Pakistan should not be in doubt about that.

Simultaneously to trying to break the ISI-LTTE nexus, the Indian government should pursue with vigour the apprehending of the LTTE supreme V. Prabhakaran and his second-in-command Pottu Amman, who are proclaimed offenders under Indian law, and who have challenged Indian sovereignty and national self-respect by assassinating a former Prime Minister, Rajiv Gandhi. The government had set up, more than two years ago, a Multi Disciplinary Monitoring Agency (MDMA) under the CBI with its primary task to hunt down Prabhakaran and Amman.

Unfortunately, the memory of the ghastly anti-Indian crime of Rajiv Gandhi's murder is getting clouded partly because of the mysteriously softening attitude of his widow and political legatee, Ms. Sonia Gandhi. Ms. Gandhi had earlier shocked the nation by asking for clemency for those LTTE-DK conspirators who had been sentenced to hang by the trial court in 1997, which was confirmed by the Supreme Court in 1999. Thereafter, she authorized her party to participate in programmes chaired by the LTTE stooge outfit, the Dravida Kazhagam (DK). The DK's leader Veeramani has been indicted by the Jain Commission in its Final Report (Part III, Volume IV, Chapter VII, pages 161-73), for abetting the LTTE in Rajiv Gandhi's murder. Ms Gandhi has also acquiesced at the least in the payment of Rs. 35 crores in ransom, by the Congress Government in Karnataka, to propitiate Prabhakaran enough to make him direct Veerappan to release Raj Kumar. And in 2004, Ms. Gandhi authorized an electoral alliance with the DMK, PMK and MDMK. That is the widow of the assassinated Rajiv Gandhi shook hands with those parties that praise the assassins (LTTE) of her husband! How can we fight terrorism if there is such abject disregard for a fallen former Prime Minister?

To effectively combat terrorism and internal security threats, we have to forge ties with China. Hostility with that country ties up our defence forces in the north, and does not permit us to shift the focus of our attention southward toward the Ocean, which in the recent centuries has been most vulnerable for our nation.

Therefore, improving relations with China should receive our best attention and effort. For this we shall have to come to a settlement on the Sino-Indian border that conforms more to our defence needs and relies less on archaic international agreements, through mutual concessions and accommodation. Such flexibility is practical in the Sino-Indian dispute. *We should face the fact that although China has no valid claim whatsoever on the border, our claims are based on the bogus documents created by the British rulers.* Let us both therefore not be prisoners of history. We need therefore, to continue and deepen our strategic dialogue with China, and remove misunderstanding on Tibet, Taiwan, Kashmir and the border, and make explicit the stand of the two ancient neighbour nations on contingencies arising out of Indo-US and Sino-Pakistan relations. Flexibility is the buzz word for China relations.

However, such flexibility is not always tenable from our national security perspective. Kashmir is the underpinning of our secular society. The UN Resolutions on Plebiscite—which was the personal folly of Pandit Nehru—or the Simla Agreement—which was the short sightedness of Mrs. Indira Gandhi,—are anyway infructuous now.

But before we can act effectively on the world stage, we must deal first and foremost with our internal security crisis. Let us recognise that due to past follies, today Kashmir is on fire. And yet hardly anyone is paying serious attention to the grave consequences for the Indian nation arising out of the situation obtaining there. Without exaggeration it can be said that Kashmir is the *agni pariksha* of the hoary concept of Indian nationhood: Kashmir stays, India survives; Kashmir secedes, India will recede. Kashmir is the negation of the vicious communal propaganda that Muslims anywhere in India will sooner or later demand another Pakistan. If Kashmir goes we shall not be able to face the onslaught of the terrorist forces elsewhere in India. India would be doomed then.

At a point of time in history, when the Soviet Union has disintegrated, Yugoslavia is in pieces, Indonesia partitioned, and Sri Lanka is in ethnic chaos, can any patriotic Indian be oblivious to the sinister developments in Kashmir and its long run consequences? The time has arrived for us to take stock. The time is now that we must devise a complete and lasting remedy to Bharat Mata's bleeding head wound that the Kashmir problem represents.

India is an ancient organic union reared in the tradition of the oldest unbroken culture in the world. Kashmir for most of India's population is not crates of cherry and beautiful carpets, but the Amarnath caves, Shankaracharya Hill and Vaishno Devi. In other words, Kashmir does not have only a Muslim population *but a hoary Hindu past.* Even the name Kashmir comes from *rishi* Kashyap who, taking the help of Brahma, Vishnu and Shiva, cleared the valley of demons by dredging the Dal Lake (see *Nilamato Purana*). Many all over India are descendents of *rishi* Kashyapa, even if they do not live in Kashmir or are Kashmiris.

If we divide Kashmir into Jammu, Ladakh and the 'Valley Plus' areas, the problem of insurgency will boil down to managing the 3 million people of the Valley. In fact, the Jammuites and the Ladakhis have been sore with the rest of India for lumping them with the Valley. In turn the Valleyites, Hindus and Muslims included, have always had contempt for them. The whole tragedy of Kashmir from the beginning is that it is the representatives of the Kashmiri Pandits who have been the villains in history; and in turn, ironically, their community is the worst victim of their own past villainy. In 1320 A.D., a Ladhaki King, Rinchana by name and Buddhist by religion, conquered the Valley, and then requested the Kashmiri Pandits to 'baptise' him to Hinduism. The Pandits refused! In a fit of anger at the insult, Raja Rinchana and his Buddhist supporters converted to Islam. In this way, Islam spread in Kashmir *not by conquest but by conversion*. Similarly, the role of Maharaja Hari Singh and his Prime Minister, R.C. Kak in creating the accession problems in 1947 by signing first a 'standstill' with India and Pakistan, are well known. Only when, faced with Pakistani intruders, he thought he would lose everything, did Hari Singh accede to India. In fact, the Kashmiri problem today is not a Hindu-Muslim question at all. It is instead a problem created by the ineffectiveness manifested by a soft state in facing the challenges of the times.

The second step to be taken by the Centre is the abolition of Article 370 of the Constitution of India. Legally, Article 370 can be abolished merely by a public notification issued by the President. It does not require Parliament's sanction, contrary to what Mr. Atal Behari Vajpayee had been telling his party workers.

Article 370 was really meant for the people of the Valley. The Jammuites and Ladakhis hate it since the Valley's elite have used Article 370 against them. Because of Article 370 a woman of Ladakh and Jammu cannot marry anyone outside the State without giving up her property rights! How can we allow such anachronisms in a modern State? Private investments from the rest of India have not been permitted in Jammu and Ladakh, where however, the local people have never felt threatened by 'invasion of Marwaris' as Nehru had claimed. In any case, the composition of the valley has been changed by the terrorists by driving out or killing the Hindu population of the Valley. This is also a violation of Article 370 since it is tantamount to changing the composition of the state.

In order to decide what to do in Kashmir, it is necessary first to define the multidimensional Kashmir problem clearly.

(*a*) *The first dimension is legal*: The creation of India and Pakistan as independent countries in August 1947 is legally founded in the Indian Independence Act enacted in June of that year by the British Parliament. In this Act there is a provision that two-thirds of the portion of the undivided India which was then under direct British rule, be partitioned into India and Pakistan. In the remaining one third of undivided India (which was indirectly ruled), the said Act revived 562 kingdoms to full sovereignty! Hitherto, these kingdoms had been under the British Crown's suzerainty and "paramountcy" from 1757, and they remained so till 1947. Section 7 of the Act caused this to lapse, and thereby restored the subjugated kingdoms to full sovereign authority. The Act read with the 1935 British India Constitution then in force, also provided that if any of the sovereigns thus empowered, chose to sign an Instrument of Accession in favour of India or Pakistan, such kingdom would be permanently merged into that country, as notified in the Instrument. There was no provision in the Act for revocation or review of the Instrument of Accession thus signed, or for the wishes of the people of any kingdom to be ascertained. That is the legal position on which modern India and Pakistan are founded.

On October 26, 1947, the Maharaja of Kashmir faced with invading irregulars, supported by the Pakistan Army, signed the Instrument of Accession in favour of India. Thus, in strictly legal terms, by virtue of the Act, the whole of Kashmir became irreversibly an inalienable part of India. Interestingly, because of this legal fact, when the matter had come before the UN the US government (judged by the declassified dispatches of the Department of State) held that India had "an iron clad legal right" to Kashmir. US delegate Mr. John Foster Dulles [as he was before becoming Secretary of State], in the UNCIP Conference in Paris in 1949 had sent dispatches to the US State Department to that effect.

The Constitution of India, moreover, does not provide for ceding any Indian territory under any circumstances. Merger into India hence is a 'one-way ticket'. Therefore by the Indian Independence Act, 1947 (from which the new nation of Pakistan draws its own legitimacy) and the Indian Constitution, once the Instrument of Accession was signed by the Maharaja of Kashmir in favour of India, there remained no legal claim of any other nation or peoples, to any part of Kashmir. In this, legally speaking, even the people of Kashmir have no voice in this merger with India. There is, therefore constitutionally speaking no scope for holding a plebiscite.

The oft-quoted Article 103 of the UN Charter has no application here since the Instrument of Accession is not a treaty, or a part of the statute that created Pakistan out of an undivided India. The UN Plebiscite Resolution of 1949 also does not recognize any right of the people of Kashmir other than the right to decide in a Plebiscite whether to be a part of India or of Pakistan. *There is no third alternative* of independent Kashmir envisaged in the UN Resolution either. Pakistan's stand has therefore been to demand self-determination by the Kashmiri people to resolve the status of Kashmir. Pakistan cleverly does not directly call for making Kashmir a part of Pakistan since there can be no legal basis for such a demand. Pakistan which controls presently about one-third of Kashmir (taken by force in 1947-48) acts as the protector of a "liberated" or Azad Kashmir. This portion has its own Prime Minister and other trappings of an independent government but without real independence. Following the 1947 merger of Kashmir with India, India had recovered two-thirds of Kashmir after sending troops to clear the Pakistan army and Pakistani infiltrators. The Gilgit portion, was denied to India by the perfidy of a British brigadier of the Indian Army, who after our jawans had captured Gilgit, hoisted the Pakistani flag and defected! Nehru acquiesced in it. Subsequently, India lost half of the secured area to China in the late 1950s when the PLA built a highway through Aksai Chin connecting Tibet with Sinkiang. By the time India woke up to it, or took notice of it, it was too late—the road had been built and the Chinese Peoples Liberation Army (PLA) vehicles were traversing to and fro. In 1962, after an incompetent attempt by Nehru to recover the area ("I have asked the army to throw the Chinese out", Nehru had said pompously) the Chinese demonstrated how determined they were to keep Aksai Chin. Thus of the total original area of Kashmir, today India, Pakistan and China have a third each of the area under their respective control.

Paradoxically, despite a decisive legal basis for our claim to Kashmir, the Indian Government has inexplicably diluted it's case on Kashmir by acknowledging that it was a "dispute" between India and Pakistan. This was admitted by India first in the United Nations in 1948. The United Nations Security Council had considered the Kashmir question only because Nehru as Prime Minister had taken the matter to the UN. Surprisingly Nehru did not have his Cabinet's approval for seeking UN intervention, but even more strange is that subsequent Indian governments have not disowned Nehru. The UN Commission on India and Pakistan (UNCIP) Resolution of January 5, 1949 that limits the proposed plebiscite choice only to accession either to India or Pakistan—and not independence for Kashmir—thus made Pakistan the sole alternative party to the dispute. Since then, the Simla Pact (1972) and the recent Agra Indo-Pak Summit (2001) reaffirmed this UN given status to Pakistan in the Kashmir dispute, and legitimized Nehru's folly.

Even the Indian Constitution (Article 370) clearly implies that Kashmir's merger with India is incomplete and unresolved. Thus, though India had an impeccable legal claim to Kashmir, we have diluted our moral right to insist on it now because of the continuous acceptance by the Indian Government of the status of Kashmir as a disputed state in which Pakistan is a party, as also by the oft-stated commitment of India to resolve the question by peaceful negotiation with Pakistan. On June 14, 2003, Deputy Prime Minister L.K. Advani for example told CNN that in order to solve the Kashmir dispute India needed to "compromise with Pakistan" and resile from its "extreme position". The legal dimension has thus evaporated and hence a future Indian government must formally repudiate; the commitment of Nehru and Mountbatten as not sanctioned by the Cabinet, and also disown Advani's unilateral concession to Washington D.C.

(*b*) *The second dimension is a moral one*: that arises from the universal concept of self-determination that is incorporated in the UN Charter.

Upon receiving India's plea, the UN had constituted a special mediatory commission (UNCIP), which passed several resolutions with the prior consent of the two countries. Two of these resolutions are important: the Cease Fire Proposal Resolution of August 13, 1948 and the Affirming Resolution of January 5, 1949. These two Resolutions are the foundation of the call for a plebiscite that is often made internationally, and to which Resolutions both India and Pakistan were willing parties (it is recorded as such in the second resolution).

It is wrong however to make out that India by these Resolutions is unconditionally committed to holding a plebiscite under UN auspices in Kashmir. India is one party to the above mentioned two Resolutions [which together may be called the Plebiscite Resolution] of UNCIP. It should be borne in mind that no Resolution that is unimplemented can be binding for forever on any government. These two

> Resolutions (designated here as R [1948] and R [1949]) are composite and contain a number of pre-conditions *on which the holding of plebiscite is contingent.* Those pre-conditions that devolve on Pakistan *have never been met*, and it is doubtful if Pakistan *can ever* meet the implied commitments embodied in the Resolutions anymore without an integral upheaval. For example, Part II(A) Clause 1 of PR (1948) states that "... the Government of Pakistan agrees to withdraw its troops from that state". Part II(A) Clause 2 amplifies this withdrawal *to include Pakistani irregulars as well.* No government of Pakistan can carry out these commitments willingly. If it could not do so in 1948, it certainly cannot now. The Clauses {Part II(B) Clause 1 read with Clause 4(*a*) of PR(1949)} moreover require to be implemented by Pakistan *prior to India taking any steps* or for the UN to schedule a plebiscite. Since Pakistan has not done so even after nearly six decades, there is no binding commitment on India to hold a plebiscite on its part.
>
> *Hence, the attempt to portray India as a country that has gone back on its international commitment to hold a plebiscite under UN auspices is simply not true: the UN resolutions on plebiscite remain dead letters today because none of the conditions precedent for its implementation obtain.* And especially so, since Pakistan, even today, would be unable to meet those conditions, constrained as it is by domestic compulsions. Hence, a solution to the Kashmir question has to be found *ab initio*, since these UN resolutions are unimplementable. The only way a solution can be found now is to simply wait. Time will provide a way. But till then the Nation must bear the expense of defending our present position against terrorism and aggression.

To meet these threats, the Nation's defence budget should be at seven per cent or thereabouts of the GDP.

According to the calculations made by the Institute of Defence Studies and Analysis (IDSA), defence expenditure since 1980 has grown at the average annual growth rate of 12.78 per cent in current prices. In the 1970s, defence expenditure grew by 10.4 per cent. In the early 1980s, between 1980/81 and 1986/87, it grew at a much higher rate of 19.5 per cent. Since then, defence expenditure has been growing at much lower rates, the average since 1986/87 being only 9.3 per cent. Since 1991, the defence expenditure has grown at 8 per cent per year. But these figures are computed in current prices, which therefore are inflated by price rises.

The differences in growth rates in defence expenditure during the past years between current prices and constant prices, are striking. During the past 20 years, Indian defence expenditure in constant price has grown only at around 5.0 per cent compared to 12.8 per cent in current prices. By sub periods, the contrast is even more blatant. During the 1970s, defence expenditure, at constant prices grew at 0.02 per cent per annum (compared to the 10.4 per cent growth in current prices). In the period between 1980/81 and 1986/87, the growth rate was much higher – 12.1 per cent. Since then it has again fallen to low levels. Between 1986/87 and 1990/91 it grew by only 2.4 per cent. And since 1991, the real or constant price defence expenditure has had negative growth rates! Thus, the Indian defence expenditure, grew substantially only between 1980/81 and 1986/87.

Defence expenditure as a percentage of GDP dropped from a high of 3.5 per cent in 1971/72 to less than 3.0 per cent in 1980/81. Thereafter it began to increase, reaching a high of 4.1 per cent in 1987/88. Since then it has been falling steadily to about 3 per cent in 1990/91 and to 2.4% in 2004. It has averaged less than 3.5 per cent in the past 20 years. It is one of the lowest in the world. This drop in the share of the defence budget is being ascribed to the resource crunch in the economy.

At a time when Pakistan is systematically fuelling armed insurrection in two border states of crucial importance to national security, and a drift to war cannot be ruled out, we cannot therefore consider a cut in our defence budget.

The defence budget of Rs. 83,000 crores (2005-2006 BE) amounted to less than 2.5 per cent of India's GDP, a low allocation for the security requirement of a vast country with extensive land and sea frontiers. Considering the extent of India's resources and interests, her expanding assets in seas beyond her shores, a defence budget of the order of 7 per cent of GDP by the year 2008 would therefore appear necessary and justifiable. The question then is how much of it should go to the Navy, Army and Air Force. Navy should get at least 30% up from the present 16% of the Budget.

Throughout her early history, India was a strong ocean oriented country. Her trade moved, as did her cultural influences, in the West as far as Egypt and Rome, and in the east to Java, Indo-China and beyond. We had a strong tradition of sea faring, of ship-building and port-construction going back to antiquity. India's sea-borne trade was a significant cause of Hindu India's famed prosperity and wealth.

The Mauryan and Gupta empires maintained sizeable navies and merchant fleets. After the disintegration of the Gupta empire, the southern kingdoms—the Satavahanas of Andhra, the Cheras of Kerala and the imperial Cholas – safeguarded and strengthened that sea-faring tradition for close to a thousand years.

Sea-power has exerted enormous influence on history in the last 600 years. It is likely to play an even more formative role in shaping the future. No great nation can play its due role in the world without the mobilisation of its maritime potential.

As already explained earlier, India has a number of the vital attributes that go into the making of a great maritime power – a strategic location stretching deep into the heart of a large ocean, a long and varied sea board with good harbours and easy access by rail, road and river, to a vast hinterland, a national aptitude for peaceful commercial pursuits, and a large population coupled with a diaspora of Indians stretching from Fiji to Guyana.

Thus far, India has long crossed technological and financial barriers to acquiring nuclear weapons. The only technological constraint now may be the lack of an adequate delivery system. The increasing expenditure on India's space programme during the last two years may be attributed to the development of intermediate range missiles capable of carrying nuclear bombs and thus remove the last technological hitch. India has already sent rockets into space and put satellites into orbit, acquiring valuable knowledge and experience which would bring India closer to the stage of having a medium range missile which could deliver a nuclear warhead. The launchers used for satellite launching could easily be converted into intermediate range ballistic missiles (IRBM). And once the Brahmos and *Surya* missile are fully operational, India will have its ICBM.

When the Prime Minister announced on May 11, 1998 the conduct of three nuclear tests, it was (despite the raw tribal euphoria that followed), essentially nothing new for informed observers of the nuclear scene. It was only a year later when the National Security Advisory Board propounded the "Indian Nuclear Doctrine" that a justification was given in terms of India developing a "minimum nuclear deterrent" with second strike capability [National Security Advisory Board: "Indian Nuclear Doctrine" Strategic Digest, *Institution of Defence Studies and Analysis* (IDSA), New Delhi, September 1999].

In 1995 the Narasimha Rao government, in an in-depth analysis by the same scientists who had ably conducted the May 11 tests, had already concluded that the available research in scholarly journals and inter-institutional academic exchanges were sufficient data, and thus all the worthwhile computer simulation could be carried out *without conducting fresh tests*.

India has thus come a long way from modern India's first Prime Minister Jawaharlal Nehru's declaration "No Bomb ever" to the thirteenth Prime Minister Mr. Vajpayee's resolve that "Sanction or No Sanction, Bomb we shall have", a transition in fifty years, ironically just as the world consensus and experience was going the other way, *viz.*, against Nehru's professed way of universal disarmament, India is going for the Bomb just as the world experience was discounting its utility.

I have no moral hatred for the Bomb as Prime Minister Morarji Desai had. In fact I can claim to be the initiator of the N Bomb national debate in the 1960s [see my "Systems Analysis of India's Strategic Needs" *Economic and Political Weekly* (Apr. 1969)]. But nevertheless I have to point out that forty years later, the ground realities and the international parameters have so substantially and dramatically changed that we may have to skin the same cat differently today. Or to use Deng Xiao Ping's phrase, the colour of the cat does not matter as long as it catches mice. What we need is, therefore, deterrence, for which alternative exist today.

The fundamental question is: Bomb for what? Does a nuclear arsenal provide sufficient deterrent worth the cost?

The question today is not whether India has the capacity or can afford it. Of course India has and can, and no one in the world anymore doubts that. The question is instead two fold:

First, producing nuclear weapons in adequate numbers with the essential delivery system to boot, to constitute a "credible minimum deterrent force" is the question. Such a credible system would entail raising our defence, atomic energy and space expenditures from the present 2.5 per cent of GDP, to at least 7 per cent of GDP. We should be clear from where the funds to meet these expenditures will come. It obviously cannot be conjured up from euphoria. Instead we shall need hard-nosed budgeting to find these resources. If any government has no intention of building a nuclear deterrent (*e.g.*, 200 bombs fitted on missiles and placed in concrete silos underground), or has no clue as to where the required funds are to be found, then the Pokharan-II tests represented adventurism and jingoism that will increase the risk of isolation and conflict, without commensurate benefit in defence.

Second, if it is the determination of the nation that the credible nuclear deterrent is to be created even if we have to forego everything (and eat grass?), then what doctrine is going to guide its use? As Prime Minister, Mr. Vajpayee had unilaterally committed to the world that India shall never be the first to use nuclear weapons. This means that our doctrine has to be based on the concept of "second strike" capability. That is, the *scenario* is that our enemy will strike first with nuclear weapons, and after we survive this attack, we shall retaliate with what is left of our arsenal. *And who is this enemy*? Pakistan? An Indo-Pakistan nuclear war is a negative sum game. Both sides will suffer irrespective of first strike by either: because the wind movements are such in the South Asian peninsula, radio-active fall out thus carried by winds will kill innocent citizens of **both** countries, no matter who drops the nuclear bomb on whom. But let it be understood, that no matter who starts the Indo-Pakistan nuclear war, New Delhi will be devastated either by the blast of an attacking Pakistan bomb or by the drifting radio active clouds from an Indian bomb dropped on Pakistan. Of course Pakistan too will die with us, but does that compensate for the devastation of our civilization? This is how interlinked we are by geography.

If a nuclear deterrent against Pakistan is a negative sum game, then is the intention of the doctrine instead to have a deterrent against China and USA? Will we be able to produce enough bombs and missiles to survive and inflict huge unacceptable damage on these two countries on a second strike, so as to deter them from making the first strike in the first place? The National Security Advisory Board's Document [2001] states as its objective that "the fundamental purpose of India nuclear weapons is to deter the use and threat of use of nuclear weapons by any state or entity (SIC) against India."

The question lies in whether we can progress in the economy sufficiently rapidly, as such a modern deterrent of such reach would require resources. Let us recall why the mighty military empire called the USSR collapsed into sixteen separate countries in 1992. From 1946, year after year, the USSR kept pace with the growing American defence technology. But its anti-individual, anti-incentive, anti-democratic ideology could not produce commensurate economic growth, so the USSR had to tighten its belt more and more every year to meet the rising cost of new technology in defence. The US President Mr. Reagan had introduced the mega-weapon Star Wars technology in 1981. To keep up with Star Wars would have required huge resources. The USSR just did not have enough resources to match that. It was thus eyeball to eyeball for fifty years; but in the end Gorbachev blinked, and opened the Pandora box of glasnost and perestroika. He tried disarmament, but his house collapsed. The USSR was dissolved thereafter.

China appears to have understood this phenomenon as early as 1982. So they abandoned their anti-US posture, and launched their economic modernization programme without reservation. During 1982-94 China has expanded at double the growth rate of India, after growing the previous 28 years (1952-81) at the same rate of growth as India's. China is thus in a position today to deploy a huge amount of resources for defence, thanks to their lying low during the 1980s and early 1990s, and building their economy.

In other words, if we are to combat China and the USA, the decision to announce our nuclear intentions should have been delayed till we have achieved a 10 per cent growth rate in the economy for about 7 years. (*i.e.*, doubling our national income thereby). Such a growth rate would wipe out unemployment in 5 years, and poverty in 10 years, besides allowing us to triple out defence budget. Thereafter, we could think in terms of global strategic nuclear policy. Rajiv Gandhi as Prime Minister had done on a smaller scale the same thing; raised the growth rate to 5 per cent above our historical 'Hindu' rate of 3 per cent, and doubled our defence budget. But alas, he had failed to grasp that foreign debt has a way of coming home to roost. The Bofors scandal and the 1990-91 payments crisis, put a stop his plans.

We could have afforded to wait for Pokharan II since we had already waited since 1964, when we first acquired the capability to explode a bomb, and more since 1974, when we had demonstrated that capability. Therefore, we could have risked waiting till AD 2010.

If India has no plan to build a holistic credible deterrent then these tests in fact have altered India's national security paradigm by cementing China-Pakistan collusion.

Hence, it is essential to know the resources requirements of India's nuclear defence system, and how India will fund the finances for it.

A nuclear weapon arsenal of *adequate* strength for second strike capability, should consist of at least 400 IRBM missiles fitted with nuclear bombs. Each such bomb will cost Rs. 1.5 crores, while the Agni missile [IRBM class] would require Rs. 15 crores each. That is, 400 IBRMs would carry a price tag of Rs. 6600 crores, plus Rs. 3500 crores for a Command, Control and Communications Centre, to monitor these missiles. This itself would cost the nation Rs. 10,100 crores. Even if we have the luxury of phasing this expenditure over two years, and before inflation and technological obsolescence overtakes this costing, the minimum per year for nuclear weaponisation would cost the nation Rs. 5050 crores. The total Defence budget provisions for fiscal 1999 for example is Rs. 5101 crores, *i.e.*, just Rs. 50 crores more than the minimum outlay for a nuclear deterrent. Obviously the decision to weaponize the nuclear capability has yet to be translated practically in terms of funding.

Perusal of the Defence Budget documents, shows that the Government is committed to the implementation of Pay Commission recommendations and Pension augmentation for defence personnel, leaving less than Rs. 1500 crores for the Capital account. This is well below the required minimum of Rs. 5050 crores annually for nuclear weapons even if the Defence Ministry spent all of the capital account provision on it, leaving nothing for conventional weapons procurement.

Therefore, the political determination of making India a "nuclear weapons state", and the claim that the Government have ordered a weaponization programme for the same, is so much hot air that should cool our adversaries, who must be reading the Indian Budget documents too.

An even more alarming picture emerges from the disaggregated capital accounts of the Budget for defence earmarked for procurement for Army, Navy and the Air Force. These allocations fall below Rs. 1500 crores as well.

This means that the re-equipment process of India's conventional armed forces weaponry have had little or no new acquisition and modernization. Considering that the rupee is continually devalued by market forces, and the weapons acquisition from abroad has to be in hard currency, even these Rs. 1500 crores shrink further in value over the fiscal years, even if this outlay was diverted wholly to conventional defence services.

There should not however be any doubt that India's armed forces urgently need updating of its weapons system besides replacement of its ageing hardware that have to be decommissioned soon. For example, during the next two years, India will lose one of the two aircraft carriers (*i.e.*, 50% reduction), a 50% loss in our frigate force from 14 vessels to 7, and a 40% de-commissioning of our submarine fleet (from 19 to 11). The Standing Committee on Defence of Parliament had opined that in order to maintain a fleet of 120 vessels for the Indian Navy, India needs to commission 6 vessels per year. And if Indian government decides to upgrade the naval reach, rather than keep the *status quo*, then a minimum of 8 new vessels would have to be commissioned every year. This is only for the Navy. The obsolescence in Air Force and Army weapons system is much faster. They require however longer periods for procurements, which has to be through hard nosed negotiations.

The current cost of an aircraft carrier is about Rs. 550 crores; that of a submarine, of tanks and aircrafts, are also exorbitant. That is why the three Defence Services Chiefs had estimated in a pre-Budget exercise in 2001 that the rock bottom Budget provision for maintaining India's armed forces *at the current levels* is 30% higher than actually budgeted by the Finance Minister. There is no rationale, therefore, for having scaled down the Defence Budget allocation any further.

Therefore, if the present Indian Government is serious about a "credible nuclear deterrent", then a considerably enhanced allocation for defence services is called for. At present, India's share in the world's defence expenditure is a mere 1.11%, when that of China is 4.16%. Of the 36 Asian countries for which we have data, India's ranking by ratio of defence expenditure to GDP, (this ratio is a mere 2.3%) is 27th, in position, while China is 13th, Pakistan is 11th. Judging by per capita expenditure on defence, India's rank is 35th at $ 8.73—beaten to the bottom of the list by Bangladesh! As far as the number of armed forces personnel per 1000 of population is concerned, India is at the bottom of the list (*i.e.*, 36th) at 1.2 per 1000, while China is 3rd at 2.42 per 1000 and Pakistan is second at 6.01 per 1000.

In fact, India's defence expenditure at constant 1980 prices, has remained stagnant since 1980 and has actually fallen since 1995. The share of defence production in that expenditure has declined from 14.8% in 1983-84 to 1.2% this year! What is significant about India's defence expenditure is that manpower costs have been rising at an annual rate of 10 per cent per year when hardware procurement budget has crawled at a mere 2 per cent per year. And over time the indigenous component of that hardware has declined to just 30 per cent. The Standing Committee of Parliament alarmed by that, had in 1996 prescribed a target for indigenous content at 70% by 2005. For this, it set the Defence R & D target expenditure at 10% of the defence outlay. But it is nowhere near that figure. In the fiscal Budget for 2005, Defence R & D is about half, at 4.9% of the defence expenditure.

The only conclusion that one can draw from all this analysis is that what the National Security Advisory Board is propounding on nuclear defence is just the contrary of what the country has budgeted for. In fact, what is of concern is that with nuclear weapons now within the reach of Pakistan, led by military generals, India's defence strategy is being formulated on the internationally disowned doctrine of second strike capability just when India must necessarily focus on a quick Israeli-type "blitzkrieg" for limited and short duration wars. The present system of defence budgeting must also be streamlined to reflect the cost effective accounting of our procurement policies *e.g.*, if we are not committed to a Blue Water Navy, why should we purchase aircraft carriers when jumbo helicopters are cheaper and more effective?

Thus, at present we may have the formal structures of a national security council and some publications on strategy, but there is in reality no well thought holistic view and no properly formulated detailed national security doctrine. This is because the formal structure lacks an ideological support framework and concept of identity.

On the principles enunciated above, the Fourth Fundamental of National Renaissance is the implementation of a national security doctrine that seeks to position India as a global power pole in a multipolar world to spread and defend Hindustan's cultural values.

6.
The Fifth Fundamental:
Sanskrit as Link Language and Devanagiri as Common Script

A society within a well defined territory is a nation only if it possesses the sentiment of nationality. Such a sentiment obtains only when there is a sense of shared historical memories and an intense longing amongst its members to live and die together. Such a sentiment can be fostered only by a factual and comprehensive understanding of history. But what is the medium for communicating these shared memories? While the authority of the State can provide the administrative cohesion for actualizing the nation, it is only when the people are able to mingle freely and communicate effortlessly with one another that the nation achieves its full bloom. This is not so today in India.

Nothing divides our nation today more than linguistic and caste differences, which over the years since independence have become more accentuated. What is more ridiculous to witness than the struggle for the city of Chandigarh, or of Belgaum on the issue of language?

The Indian people are across the regions communicating with one another today in a foreign language, which is English. This has not come to be by accident, but by a deliberate decision of Lord Macaulay in 1835. In his now famous Minute he stated: "We must at present do our best to form a class who may be interpreters between us and the millions whom we govern, a class of persons, Indians in blood and colour, but English in taste, in opinions, morals and in intellect". For this to happen Macaulay advocated that the English language should be foisted and fostered amongst this class of Indians. Although English is a language worth knowing today because the United States has made it an international language, especially for scholars, diplomats, and businessmen in the export-import & outsourcing trade, it is nevertheless not a live language for us. The nuances, the idioms, and metaphors of this language are made abroad. We have to accept these without question. If we improvise these locally, they are made fun of, and derided. How can we therefore communicate with each other in a language which we have imported from over 8000 kilometers away and kept here essentially in a mummified form?

During the freedom struggle, Hindi was proposed as a replacement for English. There was much merit in the choice because in one form or another, Hindi was understood by nearly three-fourths of India. From Kashmir to Hubli (in Karnataka), from Kutch to the corners of Assam, Hindi is an easily understood language. Only some areas of Andhra and Karnataka, and most parts of the States of Kerala and Tamil Nadu do not follow Hindi. But since Mahatma Gandhi and Rajagopalachari propagated the cause of Hindi as the link language in place of English, even these southern areas had enthusiastically begun to learn Hindi. This lasted till Gandhiji's assassination. After that, the cause of Hindi began to suffer.

There are two reasons for the decline in the spread of Hindi. First, Hindi began to be promoted by native Hindi speakers such as Purushottamdas Tandon and Dr. Raghuvira, unlike in the past when Gandhiji and Rajaji, whose mother tongue was not Hindi, were leading the campaign. The native Hindi speakers were so virulent in their campaign for the language that they became purists. They were soon perceived as fanatics. Unfortunately, these enthusiasts made the acceptance of Hindi a test of patriotism, and sought to raise knowledge of Hindi immediately as a minimum qualification for jobs. This naturally caused a deep and virulent reaction. Second, Jawaharlal Nehru as Prime Minister did nothing to dispel these negative campaigns. His heart was not in Hindi replacing English. He himself spoke a pedestrian version of Hindi, styled as Hindustani. His grandchildren Rajiv and Sanjay Gandhi were sent to the English-medium hothouse of Indo-English culture, the Doon School, which produces even today the alienated elite crowd. Nehru had digs at Hindi whenever he was afforded a chance. In Nehru's coterie it was fashionable to deride Hindi literature as consisting of just two works: Tulsidas' Ramayana and the Railway Time Table! Since Nehru understood no Sanskrit at all, he debunked the Sanskritization of the Hindi vocabulary and the Devanagiri script.

Between Raghuvira on one extreme and Nehru's sabotage on the other, Hindi became not only discredited in the eyes of the south but another imagined symbol of imposition of the North on the South. Naturally, the South revolted. Southerners also feared losing jobs due to the natural disadvantage of not knowing Hindi from childhood, in competition with those whose mother-tongue was Hindi. Thus, the nation had to witness the language riots of 1965 that threatened national unity. The leadership at the centre which had by then passed into Lal Bahadur Shastri's hands, had naturally to yield, to keep national unity, but with that the prospects of Hindi suffered a tremendous reverse.

Hindi, however, is still practically speaking the best link language today. But it is not the best language as an educational medium and for learned discourse. It can never be accepted as the national language. In the centuries to come, it is Sanskrit that will be the most suitable language for us. For fostering, nurturing, and cementing the Hindustani unity and identity. There are three reasons for this.

First, the rich literature in Sanskrit is the fount of our cultural heritage. Hindu religious ceremonies are impossible without the recitation of mantras in Sanskrit. It is already one of our 18 "national languages" in the Eighth Schedule of the Constitution. Sanskrit is the mother tongue of about 50,000 people according to the 1991 census results (Census of 2001 on language are not published yet). In 1991, more than 90 per cent of the 49,733 who returned Sanskrit as their mother tongue, were from Uttar Pradesh. Those others whose mother tongue was Sanskrit were in Bihar (802 persons), Karnataka (695), Madhya Pradesh (650), Delhi (587), Haryana (575), Rajasthan (433), Maharashtra (277), Andhra Pradesh (199), Tamil Nadu (169) and Himachal Pradesh (167). In the remaining states and union territories, the number of those who returned Sanskrit as their mother tongue was less than 100 with the lowest being one each in Tripura and Nagaland. In 1991, 56 per cent of those whose mother tongue was Sanskrit were men and 86 per cent of them lived in rural areas. Despite the low numbers of those whose mother tongue is Sanskrit, the language nevertheless has an unquestionable all India presence. It was this all-India character of the language, and the existence of Sanskrit words in large number in all Indian languages that made British imperialists target, denigrate and marginalize Sanskrit as a link language.

Hence, Thomas Babington Macaulay (1800-1859) believed that "a single shelf of a good European library was worth the whole native literature of India and Arabic". But this did not stop scholars from praising Sanskrit. Max Mueller (1823-1900) who first printed and published the Rigveda called Sanskrit the "greatest language" of the world.

Sir William Jones compared Sanskrit with the classical languages of Europe and declared in 1786, "The language of Sanskrit, whatever be its antiquity, is of the wonderful structure; more perfect than the Greek, more copious than the Latin and more exquisitely refined than either...." C. Rajagopalachari is reported to have remarked that Sanskrit was a "symbol of our seniority among peoples of the world". Among the languages that started developing a literature in the pre-Christian era, Sanskrit is the only one that continues as a living language. The languages of Egypt, Mesopotamia, Asia Minor, Syria and Carthage are only historical names in history now.

The new socio-religious movements of the 19th century among Hindus, however, did not find Sanskrit of much use to mobilize the masses. It became the second language of the Arya Samajists. The founder of the Arya Samaj, Swami Dayanand Saraswati, began spreading his gospel in Sanskrit. Swami Dayanand became an ardent supporter of Hindi as well, called it the "Arya Bhasa" and wrote all his later works in it.

Swami Dayanand's ardent disciple, Swami Shardhanand, established a gurukul at Kangri in Haridwar. The teaching in Gurukul Kangri from the primary to the university level was done in Hindi, not Sanskrit. But the Hindi was fully of sanskritized vocabulary.

Bengali is proudly referred to as the "daughter" of Sanskrit, but Tamil which has a proud history of its own, thanks to the long unbroken reign of the Chola Kingdoms, can be easily thought of as the "sister" of Sanskrit. For this reason, Sanskritized Hindi is easier to understand for the Southerners (and more difficult for those Northerners like Nehru steeped in Urdu). The late Annadurai used to say that for Sanskritized Hindi, "na vadiyar" (I am teacher). Incidentally, the Tamil word "vadiyar" comes from the Sanskrit word "vadi" (preacher). For this reason of common vocabulary, Sanskrit is ultimately the best national language for India.

Secondly, international research in today's most advanced area of computers, namely, Artificial Intelligence, which is to revolutionize the knowledge systems of the 21st Century is now increasingly coming to the conclusion that Sanskrit is the best language to store knowledge in a computer. Writing in the spring 1985 issue of *Artificial Intelligence*, Dr. Rick Briggs of the US National Aeronautics and Space Agency (NASA), states in an article titled "Knowledge Representation in Sanskrit and Artificial Intelligence" that:

"In the past twenty years, much time, effort, money has been expended on designing an unambiguous representation of natural languages to make them accessible to computer processing.

Understandably, there is widespread belief that natural languages are unsuitable for the transmission of many ideas that artificial languages can render with great precision and mathematical rigour.

There is at least one language, Sanskrit.... (in which) can be reckoned a method ..... that is identical not only in essence but in form with current work in Artificial Intelligence.

This article demonstrates that a natural language (Sanskrit) can serve as an artificial language also, and that much work in Artificial Intelligence has been reinventing a wheel millennia old".

Artificial Intelligence will revolutionize all sciences in another fifty years and Sanskrit is the best language for it. It is a pity that we Indians, the inventors of Sanskrit, have to learn these facts from foreigners, but it is better late than never.

Three decades after trying to make natural languages compatible to computer programming, scientists have begun to realize that they were beaten to it 2,600 years ago. Though much removed in time, space and culture, a 7th century B.C. Sanskrit grammarian seems to have provided all the answers to today's computer problems: that Sanskrit is well suited for encrypting without ambiguity.

The grammarian Panini is now being called the first software man, without the hardware. And the focus is on the roughly 4,000 rules of Sanskrit grammar that he evolved. Rules that are so scientific and logical in manner that they closely resemble structures used by computer scientists throughout the world.

How does Panini's grammar work? Grammar is basically an abstraction of the language. As a rule, grammar is usually written after a language has developed. Sanskrit has other forms of grammar, but Panini's is the only one which with only 4,000 rules, successfully covers almost the entire range. And each word under the Panini grammar can be traced back to its root, quite akin in form and essence to computer language like say COBOL or FORTRAN

In a natural language, for instance English, ambiguity is inherent in a large number of utterances. A crude example would be the word "bank" – as in a river bank, or a commercial bank. Another hindrance is syntax which for all intents and purposes, is independent of meaning. So computer scientists would like to eliminate such ambiguity. Scientists say the degree to which a language sounds ambiguous and cumbersome is the degree to which that language is "natural" and deviates from precise or "artificial".

But Panini has made Sanskrit precise, concise and complete. It is like a set of condensed codes for the entire language with some rules attached. It is a terse, very condensed form of Sanskrit, which paradoxically at times becomes so abstruse that a commentary is necessary to clarify it. But the beauty of it is that it can formulate logical relations in the language with scientific precision. Panini, scientists point out, can be conceived like a computer that generates correct words/sentences with the basic inputs. The computer taking the inputs uses the Panini rules and flashes the correct words or sentences in a logical order.

Scientists have gone a step forward. They are trying to develop computer-friendly grammar, like Panini, for other languages. All languages have universal rules like all of them have nouns, pronouns, verbs, adjectives etc. Effort is on to work out a Panini model for many languages. Since Sanskrit is said to be the mother of many modern Indian languages, scientists are trying to develop a mathematical and computational grammar for them. These are "catchy ideas" in artificial intelligence today, with pioneering work now being done in India, US and Germany.

Interestingly, many scientists are tempted to speculate how Panini developed his rules in so concise and precise a manner without a computer in 3995 aphorisms in his Ashtidhyayi.

Thus, as we look back, it seems that the founding fathers committed a blunder in not according Sanskrit its rightful place.

In India's long history Sanskrit has been the greatest integrating force, the source of cultural continuum, the medium of literary creativity, the voice of the sages and the languages of the most sublime thoughts and the profoundest of the philosophies of life. It was the medium of intellectual and spiritual discourse and made its impact on scholars throughout the length and breadth of the country.

It is not generally known that in the Constituent Assembly, there was a body of opinion that strongly advocated the adoption of Sanskrit as the official language (see Subhash Kashyap "Back to Sanskrit", The Hindu, Jan. 11, 2000 p. 21)). And, it is not only in India: Sanskrit had its impact in many countries outside. It became the language of the learned even in South-East Asia and to some extent in parts of Central Asia. Most interestingly, many of the ancient Sanskrit plays that exist were found not in India but in Turfan on the edge of the Great Gobi desert in China.

The highly articulate member of the Constituent Assembly, Prof. Naziruddin Ahmad, regretted that we did not know with what great veneration Sanskrit was regarded in the civilized world outside. Ahmad called Sanskrit the "greatest, grandest and the best of all languages" (quoted in Bhupendra Yadav: "Decline of Sanskrit" *Economic and Political Weekly* Dec. 31, 2005 p. 5539. He quoted W.C. Taylor who said that Sanskrit was the language of unrivalled richness and purity. Max Mueller had called Sanskrit "the greatest language in the world, the most wonderful and the most perfect."

According to Sir William Jones, "Sanskrit is of a wonderful structure, more perfect than Greek, more copious than Latin, more exquisitely refined than either." Prof. Sahibdullah, world-renowned scholar of Sanskrit, had said that Sanskrit was "the language of every man to whatever race he may belong."

Prof. Naziruddin Ahmad told the Constituent Assembly that Sanskrit was the grandest and the greatest language and was impartially difficult for all. It should therefore be accepted as India's national language in preference to Hindi which gave undue advantage to Hindi speaking areas. "If the non-Hindi people have to learn a language, they would rather learn Sanskrit than a language which is infinitely below Sanskrit in status, quality and rank."

Lakshmi Kant Maitra moved an amendment to the language clause in the Constituent Assembly. He proposed that Sanskrit should be accorded the status of the national and official language of India. He said, if on the attainment of freedom, India wanted to have anything like an official language which was also to be the national language, it could undoubtedly be only Sanskrit which was a "world language in the sense that its importance, its wealth, its position, its grandeur have made it transcend the frontiers of India and travel far beyond India, and it is because of the Sanskrit language and all the rich heritage of Indian culture that is enshrined in it that outside India we are held in deep esteem by all countries."

Maitra made a forceful plea in favour of Sanskrit as he felt that Sanskrit had "the oldest and the most respectable pedigree of all the languages in the world.

The adoption of Sanskrit, Maitra argued, would also avoid the acrimonious feelings and jealousies and accusations that would arise when a provincial language was sought to be raised to the status of a national language. He referred to the adoption of Hebrew as the official language by Israel to "show respect to their ancient language, culture and civilization and their heritage." By adoption of Sanskrit, India also could revive its ancient glories and give her message to the West – the message of the Vedas, Upanishads, Gita Varahamihira, Charaka and Susruta. It is through the message of spiritual life alone that India could regain its position of glory. Adoption of Sanskrit would give India a great chance to shape our future generations and to let the world know that we also know how to respect the rich heritage of our spiritual culture.

However, what came out of all that discussion in the Constituent Assembly was that Sanskrit was included in the Eighth Schedule of the Constitution as one of the Indian languages (the number of these languages has now gone up to 18). Also, it was provided that Hindi, which was to be the official language, would be developed by drawing wherever necessary for its vocabulary primarily from Sanskrit. This was hardly a fair deal to Sanskrit.

Nehru himself continued to pretend reverence for Sanskrit. While speaking on a Private Member's Bill in 1959, Nehru inter alia said that people grew from their roots. India had a history of 5,000 to 10,000 years. Language was a symbol of continuity. The language to which most Indian languages were connected was Sanskrit. But it was lip service. In reality Nehru sabotaged the cause of Sanskrit.

In fact, Sanskrit has made a most significant contribution to the development of all the Indian languages. With the exception of the four major languages of the South, almost all the major Indian languages had their source and derived their sustenance from Sanskrit. The languages of the South also had a large part of their vocabulary derived from Sanskrit.

The greatest resistance to Hindi being made the official language of the Union of India was based on the ground that it would mean an inbuilt advantage to those having Hindi as their mother tongue and put the others at a disadvantage. If Sanskrit is made today the official language, it will have several advantages:

1. Since Sanskrit is not the mother tongue in any State or for any group of people, it will provide an even playing field to everyone with equal advantages or disadvantages. If anything, it could have been more welcome in the South where there were many more Sanskrit scholars than elsewhere.
2. Sanskrit is a more scientific and phonetic language. As recent studies have shown, it is also the most computer-friendly.
3. Sanskrit literature is one of the richest in the world.
4. As the official language, Sanskrit will become the greatest cementing force for national unity and integration, of languages and conservation, in promotion of renaissance of Indian culture and values.
5. Sanskrit was accepted as the mother of all the languages in what philology refers to as the Indo-European Group of Languages. A large number of words in the modern European languages are derived from Sanskrit.

Also nearer home in south and south-east Asia, Bhasha Indonesia, Bhasha Malaysia, Thai, Khmer Rouge and Sinhalese are close to Sanskrit in many ways and have a large common vocabulary. The close links between the languages of Central Asia like that of Uzbekistan and Sanskrit are well known. Recent excavations in Uzbekistan have brought to light old Sanskrit inscriptions and manuscripts dating back to the beginning of the Christian era. If we want a renaissance of values and a revival of tested cultural values in our land, we should return to Sanskrit.

Not only is Sanskrit the most efficient language of the 21st Century, but its script, Devanagiri, is also the most scientific in reproducing exact sounds. Write any sentence in English; then re-write the Hindi or Sanskrit translation in Devanagiri script, and you will find that in general the latter will take up about 25 per cent less space. It is, therefore surprising to listen to the persistent demand to write Hindi in Roman (*i.e.*, English) script. On the contrary there should be an international campaign, (even if it may take a century to fructify) to make Devanagiri the international script as well. And why not? After all, numerals and decimals were accepted from Hindustan by the whole world. As British scholar Sir William Jones observed: "Our English alphabets and orthography are disgracefully, almost ridiculously, imperfect (compared to Devanagiri).

Anti-Hindi zealots confuse Devanagiri with Hindi. The truth is that Hindi is just one of the languages using this script. Sanskrit, Marathi, Sindhi, Nepali, and some of the hill tract languages also use Devanagiri. This script thus can be used by any language. In fact, the scripts of all Indian languages including Tamil and *Devanagiri* are "sisters" and direct descendants of the original *Brahmi* script. Any competent linguist would tell you that [see I. Mahadevan: *Corpus of the Tamil-Brahmi script*]. However, fanaticism blinds logic. The Punjabi (non-Sikh) Hindu under the leadership of Lala Jagat Narain had two decades ago launched a bitter campaign against the *Gurumukhi* script. To avoid being forced to use Gurumukhi they even declared that their language is Hindi and not Punjabi although they spoke the latter. This was out of misguided exuberance—because the *Gurumukhi* script is very similar to the *Devanagiri* script, just as the Gujarati script is. Anyone who knows *Devanagiri* can master Gurumukhi in 24 hours. Yet a senseless agitation took place, followed by an unhealthy polarization process that culminated in Operation Bluestar in 1984, the tragic aftereffects of which we feel even today.

The point is that even if *Devanagiri* is the most scientific phonetic script ever invented, for practical reasons there is every reason to respect the scripts of other Indian languages. In a calm dispassionate atmosphere which may take decades to attain, young people, especially those entering primary and secondary schools, will learn at least two languages and two scripts: (1) mother tongue and Sanskrit and (2) own script and Devanagiri. In the meantime,

Hindi should continue to Sanskritize itself to the point where it becomes almost indistinguishable from Sanskrit. It will then merge into Sanskrit, disappearing excepting in local dislects. Sanskrit was once long ago uprooted from India by Pali. But after some centuries, this versatile language was rethroned by the same process via Mahayana Buddhism. A second rethroning of Sanskrit can now be achieved through Hindi. Till that day, if the three languages formula, which requires northerners to learn one southern language, is sincerely implemented, we can make a steady progress towards the goal of making Sanskrit once again the national language of India. Already 70 lakh students are currently studying Sanskrit, more than 200 universities in 35 countries offer courses in it. It may take years to accomplish that but we must commit ourselves to that goal now. We should also commit ourselves to see that no language, especially Urdu, suffers because of the dominance of Sanskrit. In day-to-day conversations, such languages will continue to flourish.

Thus, on the Agenda for Renaissance, the Fifth Fundamental would be to unite the nation by propagating for adoption of Sanskrit as the ultimate national language of India and Devanagiri as a compulsory alternative script for all Indian languages. For the time being, Hindi vocabulary should be continually sanskritized till Hindi itself merges into Sanskrit.

Index